THE
SCIENCE
OF GETTING
RICH

WITH
THE SCIENCE OF
BEING GREAT

Wallace D. Wattles

Edited, Modernized, and Updated for the 21st Century by Arthur R. Pell, Ph.D.

FiNGERPRINT!

Published 2025

FiNGERPRINT!
Prakash Books

 Fingerprint Publishing
 @FingerprintP
 @fingerprintpublishingbooks
www.fingerprintpublishing.com

© JMW Group, Inc.
jmwgroup@jmwgroup.net
jmwforlife.com
Rights licensed exclusively by JMW Group Inc.

ISBN: 978 93 8943 292 3

INTRODUCTION

In the popular musical *Fiddler on the Roof*, Tevya, the dairyman, sings the plaintive song, 'If I were a rich man . . .' How often have you dreamed that you were wealthy and could live a life of luxury? Wealth seems so remote to most people, yet there are countless examples throughout history of men and women who by their own efforts rose from the depths of poverty to great riches.

Others dream of being a great person – one to whom friends, neighbors, and even strangers look up to for leadership and guidance. Greatness is in the grasp of every human being. If only they reached out for it.

From ancient times, philosophers have pondered over the puzzle of how some seemingly average men and women have burst out from the common crowd into wealth or greatness. What was the secret of their success?

Several deep thinkers in the late nineteenth and early twentieth century studied this phenomenon and preached, wrote and practiced a new way of looking at life. By combining a metaphysical, spiritual and pragmatic approach to the way we think and live, they uncovered the secret of attaining what we truly desire.

This philosophy was not a religion in the traditional sense, but it was based on an unconditional belief in a higher being, an eternal presence, God. It was called by various names such as 'New Thought' and 'New Civilization.'

The proponents of the New Thought or New Civilization preached a new idea of life that brings out new methods and more perfected results. They base their thinking on the concept that the human soul is linked with the atomic mind of universal substance, which links our lives with the universal law of supply and we have the power to use it to enrich our lives. To achieve our goals, we must work for it, and this working, we may suffer the thorns and heartaches of humankind. We can do all these things only as we have found the law and worked out the understanding of the law, which God seemed to have written in riddles in the past.

In the ages gone by, we did not know how to sail the seas, or tunnel the earth, or conquer the air, nor was there a botanist like Luther Burbank to teach the crossing of natural laws, or a Marconi or Tesla, to show us we can learn to use the invisible airwaves. As soon as we knew more, we expressed more, and today all these things are made plain. In the law of psychological consciousness there have arisen psychological Burbanks and Marconis, who are working with unseen natural laws, bringing the human mind out into newfound expressions of conscious power.

We know that our consciousness is always united with the consciousness of God, or universal mind, and that all possession in form comes through recognition in mind.

The old civilization taught that all external conditions came as the result of external action and that poverty was the polar opposite of wealth and was the result of the rich taking supply away from the poor. It saw an individual's line of transference blocked by the greed of another. Through old-thought centuries humankind believed this inversion of the truth and crept on in resistance, strife and condemnation, never knowing where to put the blame. From this false premise of reasoning there came all the tyranny and bloodshed of the past. But today a veil of consciousness has lifted, and the new thinkers see life in its entirety and not just the components of it.

No matter what we want, we will find that comprehension. We can get it if we are willing to pay the price, not always in our way, but in the way that will bring us toward the thing for which we have asked. Left to our own way we would now and then go in a directly opposite path from our desires, for we cannot see the end from the beginning, but once we have made the consecration, if we find the path rough and winding, we cannot choose but go on.

No greater good can come to any man or woman than to become self-active. All the experiences of life are designed by Providence to force men and women into self-activity; to compel them to cease being creatures of circumstances and master their environment. In the lowest stage of our lives, we are children of chance and circumstance and the slave of fear. Our acts are all reactions resulting from the impingement upon us of forces in our environment. We act only as we are acted upon. We originate nothing. But within themselves a Principle of Power sufficient to master all that they fear and if they learn this and become self-active, they become as one of the gods.

Nothing was ever in any human being that is not in you; no one ever had more spiritual or mental power than you can attain, or did greater things than you can accomplish. The New Thought concept can be summed up in these words:

You can become what you want to be.

All that we achieve and all that we fail to achieve is the direct result of our own thoughts. In a justly ordered universe, where loss of balance would mean total destruction, individual responsibility must be absolute. Our weaknesses and strengths, purity and impurity are ours alone and that of another person. They are brought about by ourselves and not by another. They can only be altered by ourselves, never by another.

All our happiness and suffering are evolved from within. As we think, so we are; as we continue to think, so we remain. The only way we can rise, conquer and achieve is by lifting up our thoughts. The only reason we may remain weak, abject and miserable is to refuse to lift up our thoughts.

All achievements, whether in the business, intellectual or spiritual world are the result of definitely directed thought, are governed by the same law and are of the same method; the only difference lies in the object of attainment. Those who would accomplish little must sacrifice little; those who would achieve must sacrifice much; those who would attain a great deal must sacrifice a great deal.

In order to live an enriched life, we must aim to achieve—

1. **A Positive Mental Attitude**

   All riches, of whatsoever nature, begin as a state of mind, and let us remember that a state of mind is the one and only thing over which any person has complete, unchallenged right of control. The Creator provided us control over nothing except the power to shape our own thoughts and the privilege of filling them to any pattern of our choice. A positive mental attitude is the starting point of all riches whether they are riches of a material nature or intangible riches.

2. **Sound Physical Health**

   Sound health begins with a health consciousness produced by a mind that thinks in terms of health and not in terms of illness, plus temperance of habits in eating and properly balanced physical activities.

3. **Harmony in Human Relationships**

   Harmony with others begins with one's self, for it is true, as Shakespeare said, "To thine own self be true, and it must follow as the night the day, thou canst not then be false to any man."

4. **Freedom from Fear**

   Fear keeps us from being truly free. Fear is a harbinger of evil, and wherever it appears one may find a cause which must be eliminated before one may become rich in the fuller sense.

5. **The Hope of Achievement**

   The greatest of all forms of happiness comes as the result of hope of achievement of some yet unattained desire.

6. **The Capacity for Faith**

   Faith is the connecting link between our conscious mind and the great universal reservoir of Infinite Intelligence. It is the fertile soil of the garden of the human mind wherein may be produced all of the riches of life. It is the 'eternal elixir' that gives creative power and action to the impulses of thought. Faith is the basis of all so-called miracles, and of many mysteries that cannot be explained by the rules of logic or science. Faith is the power that transmutes the ordinary energies of thought into their spiritual equivalent.

7. **Willingness to Share One's Blessings**

   Happiness comes only by sharing. All riches may be embellished and multiplied by the simple process of sharing them where they may serve others. Riches that are not shared, whether they are material or intangible riches, wither and die like the rose on a severed stem, for it is one of nature's first laws that inaction and disuse lead to decay and death, and this law applies to our material possession just as it applies to the living cells of every physical body.

8. **A Labor of Love**

   There can be no richer person that one who has found a labor of love and is busily engaged in performing it. Labor is the liaison between the demand and supply of all human needs, the forerunner of all progress, the medium by which our imagination is given the wings of action. And the labor of love is sanctified because it brings the joy of self-expression to those who perform it.

9. An Open Mind on All Subjects

Tolerance, which is among the higher attributes of culture, is expressed only by those who hold an open mind on all subjects at all times. And it is only those with open minds who become truly educated and who are prepared to avail themselves of the greater riches of life.

10. Self-Discipline

Unless we are masters of ourselves, we may never become master of anything. The highest form of self-discipline consists in the expression of humility of the heart when one has attained great riches or has been overtaken by that which is commonly called 'success.'

11. The Capacity to Understand People

We must recognize that all people are fundamentally alike in that they have evolved from the same stem. To understand others, we must first understand ourselves. The capacity to understand others eliminates many of the common causes of interpersonal frictions. It is the foundation of all friendship. It is the basis of all harmony and cooperation among people. It is the fundamental ingredient of great leadership in that it calls for friendly cooperation.

12. Economic Security

You have the right to become economically secure — even really rich. However, economic security is not attained by the possession of money alone. It is attained by the service one renders, for useful service may be converted into all forms of human needs with or without the use of money.

In the following pages, you will learn the secrets of attaining wealth and greatness. Part I of this book will deal with wealth.

You will learn the secret of how to change your mindset from accepting the condition of poverty to a forward thinking, positive approach to achieving your heart's desire. Part II will cover how to move above the crowd to be a truly respected and admired person, a leader among your peers, in short, a great person.

Caution: Reading this book will not make you rich or great. Wishing will not make it happen. You will reach your goals only by putting into practice the concepts you learn here.

Arthur R. Pell, Ph.D., Editor
November 2005

CONTENTS

PART I

THE SCIENCE OF GETTING RICH

PREFACE

Are you destined to be poor? To paraphrase Shakespeare, some people are born wealthy, some achieve wealth, and some have wealth thrust upon them. There are some among us who were fortunate to have wealthy parents, who gave us all that money could buy — but many of these people have lost their parent's wealth through their own bad judgments. There are others who had wealth thrust upon them by winning a lottery or some other windfall. However, most of us are not so lucky. In order to become wealthy, we have to achieve through our own intelligence, diligence, creativity and commitment. None of us are destined to be poor. Wealth is all around us and all we need do to achieve it is to seek and follow the road that will lead us there.

These proponents of the New Thought or New Civilization preach a new idea of life that brings out new methods and more perfected results. They base their thinking on the concept that the human soul is linked with the atomic mind of universal substance, which links our lives with the universal law of supply and we have the power to choose over which line it shall manifest for us. To achieve our goals, we must work for it, and with this working suffer the thorns and heartaches of humankind. We can do all these things only as we have found the law and worked out the understanding of the law, which God seemed to have written in riddles in the past.

In the ages gone by, we did not know how to sail the seas, or tunnel the earth, or conquer the air, nor was there a botanist like

Luther Burbank to teach the crossing of natural laws, or a Marconi or Tesla, to show us we can learn to use the invisible airwaves. As soon as we knew more, we expressed more, and today all these things are made plain. In the law of psychological consciousness there have arisen psychological Burbanks and Marconis, who are working with unseen natural laws, bringing the race mind out into newfound expressions of conscious power.

We know that our consciousness is always united with the consciousness of God, or universal mind, and that all possession in form comes through recognition in mind.

The old civilization taught that all external conditions came as the result of external action and that poverty was the polar opposite of wealth and was the result of the rich taking supply away from the poor; it saw an individual's line of transference blocked by the greed of another. Through old-thought centuries the human race believed this inversion of the truth and crept on in resistance, strife and condemnation, never knowing where to put the blame. From this false premise of reasoning there came all the tyranny and bloodshed of the past. But today a veil of consciousness has lifted, and the new thinkers see life in its entirety and not in the part.

All life is a school and each life is in its own grade; poverty is simply the lesson of one grade, riches the lesson of another. There are millions of people on this planet today who are poor because they have not evolved to where they are able to conquer supply.

The first step in the grade for the poverty-stricken is to learn to conquer supply and this conquest is brought about not from without but through the slow process of awakening individual perception; which neither the race nor the individual can outstrip.

As soon as they have learned this lesson they pass on into the next grade where they learn how to use wealth, and their place is immediately taken by another learning the old lesson.

The New Civilization knows that there are *now, and always* will be some people who accept poverty as their natural portion. However, they are not doomed to that state because the tools are there to help them lift themselves from this state by increasing development and understanding.

Those who know life understand this *first cause of poverty*. When we look more deeply we see that until the last person of this and similar groups has died out, the poverty stricken will continue to be in our midst, because deep in their minds and souls they still look upon themselves as beggars.

The second cause of poverty is the false education of the past, which, instead of hastening the evolution of humankind, has served to keep it in bondage. Many religions contain as part of their dogma that poverty is an inevitable condition for most people. They preach, 'The poor will always be with us.' Some sects even claim that for many, poverty is predestined and should be accepted as a way of life.

The old civilization was too undeveloped to think for itself and so for ages it accepted the thought-force of its religious and secular leaders. People built their lives to express these beliefs. As long as we believed in two forces – God and devil spirit and matter – we received these things, for 'there is nothing in all this world but thinking makes it so.' Held in the bondage of the old thoughts and beliefs, we created and re-created our own lack, limitations, disease and poverty.

Under these teachings the multitude developed a poverty-stricken cringing consciousness, and everything in form being projected from the inner states of consciousness, it could not escape the law it set in operation for itself, and lack, crime, disease and abject poverty came the heritage of the human race.

The human race was taught that to be poor was to be spiritual, that it was 'easier for the camel to go through the eye of a needle than for a rich person to enter the kingdom of Heaven.' Living in the lie of a futurity they suffered on in misery, hoping and trusting that in some far-off future day, a heaven (if they deserved it by their faithful poverty) would be given them for their pain. In some religions such as those of the East, persons born in poverty will always live in poverty – hoping that by being obedient and humble, they will be reborn in their next life in a higher caste and more affluent life.

These old obsessions of race thought and race interpretation held the multitude in their iron clasp for centuries. Strange as it may seem, even now in the very center, of an enlightened century, there are still many minds hugging to their hearts this old delusion and dragging on in penury and despair, resisting the compelling force of higher revelation.

There are thousands, today poor, who still cling to this old tradition, only from false religious ardor and lack of self-investigation.

Another obsession of the old civilization is the one of inheritance. It *is* yet said by those who should know better: 'Oh, I am born to be poor.' They are born to be poor only as long as they will not, do not, or cannot, learn the law of supply. While there are many who are born to be poor in understanding, there are thousands who are fast working through their grade and are ready to come out into a new action of the law. The power to stand still under a law, or to go on into relationship with another is within ourselves, but not knowing this, we stand still, accepting an old condition as binding, when within ourselves there is the awakening power for freedom.

The New Civilization brings a new message and there are many millions in these days who are out into a new kingdom of thought, bringing new laws into operation in their environment.

We are poor and will stay poor only as long as we relate with the laws of poverty; success, wealth and supply can be planned for by every life just as scientifically as one can build a house or plan a city.

Supply cannot refuse to come to any of us who set a supply law into operation; but we must be taught this law and brought step by step away from the old ideas and obsessions of the past into a new understanding and use of new methods.

Poverty and wealth are the results of internal states of mind and only as mind changes will material change.

There are childish states of consciousness that operate against material harmony; worry, hate, fear, anxiety and condemnation are interior pivots for exterior hovels and wherever we rest our ideas and energies, substance must gather round.

A mind that has been poised through incarnations in the belief of poverty and its power, and backs this belief in the present with childish states of mind – anger, worry and fear will find poverty abiding with it.

Environment is only a big mirror in which we see ourselves reflected. People who depend on charities for their meals or who sleep on the benches in the park, are doing so, not because circumstances force them to it, but because of their own ignorant manipulation of the laws, they have forced the circumstances.

Poverty will remain only as long as we have within ourselves the germ that intensifies it, and we will secure wealth and freedom only as we grow into it out from the natural states of our minds and hearts.

We are poor because we do not know any better than to be poor. We stay poor because we are too ignorant, too weak or too inert, or, too superstitious to hold our life servant to the higher laws of life and compel a new physical arrangement, by an ever-increasing recognition of our own God-power.

When we can fully and actually incorporate into our minds the consciousness of infinite supply, and our inseparable connection with it, we may let go everything we have in the world and make instantaneous relation with the lines that will lead us again into abundance.

This does not mean that we can sit down with our hands folded and expect miracles to be performed for us; money does not manifest without material lines of transference. We have to work in scientific manner to achieve wealth. In the following chapters, you will learn the step-by-step scientific approach to attaining wealth. Read it and apply it to your lives.

Chapter

1

THE RIGHT TO BE RICH

Whatever may be said in praise of poverty, the fact remains that it is not possible to live a really complete or successful life unless one is rich. We cannot rise to our greatest possible height in talent or soul development unless we have plenty of money. In order for us to unfold the soul and to develop talent we must have many things to use, and we cannot have these things unless we have money to buy them.

We develop in mind, soul, and body by making use of things, and society is so organized we must have money in order to become the possessor of things; therefore, the basis of all advancement must be the science of getting rich.

The object of all life is development; and all things that live have an inalienable right to all the development it is capable of attaining.

Our right to life means our right to have the free and unrestricted use of all the things which may be necessary to our fullest mental, spiritual, and physical development; or, in other words, our right to be rich.

This book will not speak of riches in a figurative way. To be really rich does not mean to be satisfied or contented with a little. We need not be satisfied with a little if we are capable of using and enjoying more. The purpose of Nature is the advancement and development of life; and all of us should have all that can contribute to the power; elegance, beauty, and richness of life; to be content with less is sinful.

Those who own all they want for the living of all the life they are capable of living are rich; and those who do not have plenty of money can have all they want. Life has advanced so far, and become so complex, that even the most ordinary man or woman requires a great amount of wealth in order to live in a manner that even approaches completeness. Every person naturally wants to become all that they are capable of becoming; this desire to realize innate possibilities is inherent in human nature; we cannot help wanting to be all that we can be. Success in life is becoming what you want to be; you can become what you want to be only by making use of things, and you can have the free use of things only as you become rich enough to buy them. To understand the science of getting rich is therefore the most essential of all knowledge.

There is nothing wrong in wanting to get rich. The desire for riches is really the desire for a richer, fuller, and more abundant life; and that desire is praise worthy. People who do not desire to live more abundantly are abnormal, and so people who do not desire to have money enough to buy all they want are abnormal.

There is no virtue in poverty. It is a mental disease that should be abolished from the face of the earth. You are here to grow, expand and develop spiritually, mentally and materially. You have the inalienable right to fully develop and express yourself along all lines. You should surround yourself with beauty and luxury.

Why be satisfied with just enough to go around when you can enjoy the riches of the infinite? In this book you will learn to make friends with money, and you will always have a surplus. Your desire to be rich is a desire for a fuller, happier and more wonderful life. It is a cosmic urge that is good – indeed, very good. Begin to see money in its true significance. It is a symbol of exchange. It means to you freedom from want, beauty, luxury, abundance and refinement.

One of the reasons many people do not have more money is that they are silently or openly condemning it. They refer to money as 'filthy lucre,' or they believe that 'love of money is the root of all evil' or similar fallacies. Another reason they do not prosper is that they have a sneaky, subconscious feeling that there is some virtue in poverty. This feeling may derive from early childhood training, superstition, of based on a false interpretation of the scriptures.

There is no virtue in poverty. It is a disease like any other mental disease. If you were physically ill, you would think there was with you and would seek help or do something about it at once. Likewise, if you do not have money constantly circulating in your life, there is something radically wrong with you.

God does not want you to live in a hovel or to go hungry. God *wants* you to be happy, prosperous and successful. God is always successful in His undertakings, whether He makes a star or a cosmos.

Get away immediately from all superstitious beliefs about money. Do not ever regard money as evil or filthy. If you do, you cause it to take wings and fly away from you. Remember that you lose what you condemn.

There are three motives for which we live; we live for the body, we live for the mind, we live for the soul. No one of these is better or holier than the other. All are alike desirable, and no one of the three – body, mind, or soul – can live fully if either of the others is cut short of full life and expression. It is not right or noble to live only for the soul and deny mind or body; and it is wrong to live for the intellect and deny body or soul.

We are all acquainted with the loathsome consequences of living for the body and denying both mind and soul; and we see that *real* life means the complete expression of all that we can give forth through body, mind, and soul. Whatever we can say, we cannot really be happy or satisfied unless our body is living fully in every function, and unless the same is true of our mind and soul. Wherever there is unexpressed possibility, or function not performed, there is unsatisfied desire. Desire is possibility seeking expression, or function seeking performance.

We cannot live fully in body without good food, comfortable clothing, and warm shelter; and without freedom from excessive toil. Rest and recreation are also necessary to our physical life.

We cannot live fully in mind without books and time to study them, without opportunity for travel and observation, or without intellectual companionship.

To live fully in mind we must have intellectual recreations, and must surround ourselves with all the objects of art and beauty we are capable of using and appreciating. To live fully in soul, we must have love; and love is denied expression by poverty.

Our highest happiness is found in the bestowal of benefits on those we love; love finds its most natural and spontaneous expression in giving. If we have nothing to give, we cannot fill our place as a spouse or parent, as a citizen, or as a human being. It is in the use of material things that we find full life for our body, develop our mind and our soul. It is therefore of supreme importance to us that we should be rich.

It is perfectly right that you should desire to be rich; if you are a normal man or woman you cannot help doing so. It is perfectly right that you should give your best attention to the Science of Getting Rich, for it is the noblest and most necessary of all studies. If you neglect this study, you are derelict in your duty to yourself, to God and humanity; for you can render to God and humanity no greater service than to make the most of yourself.

Chapter

2

THERE IS A SCIENCE OF GETTING RICH

There is a Science of getting rich, and it is an exact science, like algebra or arithmetic. There are certain laws that govern the process of acquiring riches; once we learn and obey these laws we will get rich with mathematical certainty.

The ownership of money and property comes as a result of doing things in a Certain Way. Those who do things in this Certain Way, whether on purpose or accidentally, get rich; while those who do not do things in this Certain Way, no matter how hard they work or how able they are, remain poor.

It is a natural law that like causes always produce like effects; and, therefore, any man or woman who learns to do things in this certain way will infallibly get rich.

That the above statement is true is shown by the following facts:

Getting rich is not a matter of environment. If it were, all the people in certain neighborhoods would become wealthy; the people of one city would all be rich, while those of other towns would all be poor; or the inhabitants of one state would roll in wealth, while those of an adjoining state would be in poverty.

But everywhere we see rich and poor living side-by-side, in the same environment, and often engaged in the same vocations. When two people are in the same locality, and in the same business, and one gets rich while the other remains poor, it shows that getting rich is not, primarily, a matter of environment. Some environments may be more favorable than others, but when two people in the same business are in the same neighborhood, and one gets rich while the other fails, it indicates that getting rich is the result of doing things in a Certain Way.

And further, the ability to do things in this certain way is not due solely to the possession of talent, for many people who have great talent remain poor, while other who have very little talent get rich.

Studying the people who have become rich, we find that they are an average lot in all respects, having no greater talents and abilities than other people. It is evident that they do not get rich because they possess talents and abilities that others do not have, but because they happen to do things in a Certain Way.

Getting rich is not the result of saving, or 'thrift'; many very penurious people are poor, while free spenders often get rich.

Nor is getting rich due to doing things which others fail to do; for two people in the same business often do almost exactly the same things, and one gets rich while the other remains poor or becomes bankrupt.

From all these things, we must come to the conclusion that getting rich is the result of doing things in a Certain Way.

If getting rich is the result of doing things in a Certain Way, and if like causes always produce like effects, then any man or woman who can do things in that way can become rich, and the whole matter is brought within the domain of exact science.

The question arises here, whether this Certain Way may not be so difficult that only a few may follow it. This cannot be true, as we have seen, so far as natural ability is concerned. Talented people get rich, and blockheads get rich; intellectually brilliant people get rich, and very stupid people get rich; physically strong people get rich, and weak and sickly people get rich.

Some degree of ability to think and understand is, of course, essential; but in so far natural ability is concerned, any man or woman who has sense enough to read and understand these words can certainly get rich.

Also, we have seen that it is not a matter of environment. Location counts for something; one would not go to the heart of the Sahara and expect to do successful business.

Getting rich involves the necessity of dealing with other people, and of being where there are people to deal with; and if these people are inclined to deal in the way you want to deal, so much the better. But that is about as far as environment goes.

If anybody else in your town can get rich, so can you; and if anybody else in your state can get rich, so can you.

Again, it is not a matter of choosing some particular business or profession. People get rich in every business, and in every profession; while their next-door neighbors in the same vocation remain in poverty.

It is true that you will do best in a business that you like, and which is congenial to you; and if you have certain talents that are well developed, you will do best in a business that calls for the exercise of those talents.

Also, you will do best in a business that is suited to your locality. An ice-cream parlor would do better in a warm climate than in Greenland, and a salmon fishery will succeed better in the Northwest than in Florida, where there are no salmon.

But, aside from these general limitations, getting rich is not dependent upon your engaging in some particular business, but upon your learning to do things in a Certain Way. If you are now in business, and anybody else in your locality is getting rich in the same business, while you are not getting rich, it is because you are not doing things in the same Way that the other person is doing them.

No one is prevented from getting rich by lack of capital. True, as you get capital the increase becomes more easy and rapid; but one who has capital is already rich, and does not need to consider how to become so. No matter how poor you may be, if you begin to do things in the Certain Way you will begin to get rich; and you will begin to have capital. The getting of capital is a part of the process of getting rich; and it is a part of the result that invariably follows the doing of things in the Certain Way.

You may be the poorest person on the continent, and be deeply in debt, but if you begin to do things in this way, you must infallibly begin to get rich. If you have no capital, you can get capital. If you are in the wrong business, you can get into the right business. If you are in the wrong location, you can go to the right location; and you can do so by beginning in your present business and in your present location to do things in the Certain Way that causes success.

Chapter

3

IS OPPORTUNITY MONOPOLIZED?

No one is kept poor because opportunity has been taken away or because other people have monopolized the wealth and have put a fence around it. You may be shut off from engaging in business in certain lines, but there are other channels open to you.

At different periods the tide of opportunity sets in different directions, according to the needs of the whole, and the particular stage of social evolution that has been reached. At the beginning of the twenty-first century in America, manufacturing and related industries are declining. But new opportunities are opening in many areas such as health care, computers and service industries.

In developing countries in Asia, Africa and South America, tremendous opportunities are opening in manufacturing and service industries. Many multinational companies are outsourcing production and even service activities to enterprising entrepreneurs in these nations. Opportunities to become rich are growing rapidly. There is abundance of opportunity for the person who will go with the tide, instead of trying to swim against it.

Nobody is deprived of opportunity. Workers are not being 'kept down' by their masters; they are not being 'ground' by conglomerates or cartels. People can move up from lower level jobs or poorly paid occupations when they begin to do things in a Certain Way. The law of wealth is the same for them as it is for all others. This they must learn; and they will remain where they are as long as they continue to do as they do. No one is kept in poverty by shortness in the supply of riches; there is more than enough for all. A palace as large as the capitol at Washington might be built for every family on earth from the building material in the United States alone. Under intensive cultivation, this country could produce wool, cotton, linen, and silk enough to cloth each person in the world finer than Solomon was arrayed in all his glory; together with food enough to feed them all luxuriously.

The visible supply is practically inexhaustible; and the invisible supply really *is* inexhaustible.

Everything you see on earth is made from one Divine Substance, out of which all things proceed.

New Forms are constantly being made, and older ones are dissolving; but all are shapes assumed by the eternal God.

There is no limit to the supply of Divine Stuff. The universe is made out of it; but it was not all used in making the universe. The spaces in, through, and between the forms of the visible universe are permeated and filled with the Divine Stuff; with the raw material of all things. Ten thousand times as much as has been made might still be made, and even then we should not have exhausted the supply of universal raw material.

No person therefore, is poor because nature is poor, or because there is not enough to go around.

Nature is an inexhaustible storehouse of riches; the supply will never run short. Divine Substance is alive with creative energy, and is constantly producing more forms. When the supply of building material is exhausted, new resources will be developed to replace them; when the soil is exhausted so that food stuffs and materials for clothing will no longer grow upon it, it will be renewed by new developments of science.

This is true of the human race collectively; the race as a whole is always abundantly rich, and if individuals are poor, it is because they do not follow the Certain Way of doing things that makes the individual rich.

The Divine Stuff is intelligent; it is stuff which thinks. It is alive, and is always impelled toward more life.

It is the natural and inherent impulse of life to seek to live more. It is the nature of intelligence to enlarge itself, and of consciousness to seek to extend its boundaries and find fuller expression. The universe of forms has been made by Divine Living Substance, throwing itself into form in order to express itself more fully.

The universe is a great Living Presence, always moving inherently toward more life and fuller functioning.

Nature is formed for the advancement of life; its impelling motive is the increase of life. For this cause, everything that can possibly minister to life is bountifully provided; there can be no lack unless God is to contradict Himself and nullify His own works.

You are not kept poor by lack in the supply of riches; it is a fact that shall be demonstrated a little farther on that even the resources of the Divine Supply are at the command of the man or woman will act and think in a Certain Way.

Chapter

4

THE FIRST PRINCIPLE IN THE SCIENCE OF GETTING RICH

Thought is the only power that can produce tangible riches from the Divine Substance. The stuff from which all things are made is a substance that thinks, and a thought of form in this substance produces the form.

Divine Substance moves according to its thoughts; every form and process you see in nature is the visible expression of a thought in this Substance. As the Divine Stuff thinks of a form, it takes that form; as it thinks of a motion, it makes that motion. That is the way all things were created. We live in a thought world, which is part of a thought universe. The thought of a moving universe extended throughout Divine Substance, and the Thinking Stuff moving according to that thought, took the form of systems of planets, and maintains that form. Thinking Substance takes the form of its thought, and moves according to the thought. Holding the idea of a circling system of suns and worlds, it takes the form of these bodies, and moves them as it thinks. Thinking the form of a slow-growing oak tree, it moves accordingly, and produces the tree, though centuries may be required to do the work. In creating, the Divine seems to move according to the lines of motion it has established; the thought of an oak tree does not cause the instant formation of a full-grown tree, but it does start in motion the forces that will produce the tree, along established lines of growth.

Every thought of form, held in thinking Substance, causes the creation of the form, but always, or at least generally, along lines of growth and action already established.

The thought of a house of a certain construction, if it were impressed upon Divine Substance, might not cause the instant formation, of the house, but it would cause the turning of creative energies already working in trade and commerce into such channels as to result in the speedy building of the house. And if there were no existing channels through which the creative energy could work, then the house would be formed directly from primal substance, without waiting for the slow processes of the organic and inorganic world.

No thought of form can be impressed upon Divine Substance without causing the creation of the form.

The human mind is a thinking center, and can originate thought. All the forms that we fashion with our hands must first exist in our thought. We cannot shape a thing until we have thought that thing.

And so far we have confined our efforts wholly to the work of our hands. We have applied manual labor to the world of forms, seeking to change or modify those already existing. We have never thought of trying to cause the creation of new forms by impressing our thoughts upon Divine Substance.

When we have a thought-form, we take material from the forms of nature, and makes an image of the form which is in our mind. We have, so far, made little or no effort to co-operate with Divine Intelligence; to work with God. We reshape and modify existing forms by manual labor, but we have given no attention to the question whether we may not produce things from Divine Substance by communicating our thoughts to it. We propose to prove that we may do so; to prove that any man or woman may do so, and to show how. As our first step, we must lay down three fundamental propositions.

First, we assert that there is one original Divine stuff, or substance, from which all things are made. All the seemingly

34

many elements are but different presentations of one element. All the many forms found in organic and inorganic nature are but different shapes, made from the same stuff – and this stuff is thinking stuff. A thought held in it produces the form of the thought. Thought, in thinking substance, produces shapes. The human mind is a thinking center, capable of original thought. If we can communicate our thoughts to original thinking substance, we can cause the creation, or formation, of the thing we think about. To summarize this—

- *There is a thinking stuff from which all things are made, and which, in its original state, permeates, penetrates, and fills the interspaces of the universe.*
- *A thought, in this substance, produces the thing that is imaged by the thought.*
- *We can form things in our thought, and, by impressing our thought upon Divine substance, can cause the thing we think about to be created.*

It may be asked if these statements can be proved. Without going into details, they can be proved by both logic and experience.

Reasoning back from the phenomena of form and thought, there is one original thinking substance; and reasoning forward from this thinking substance, we derive our power to cause the formation of the thing we think about.

If one person who reads this book gets rich by doing what it recommends, that is evidence in support of this claim; but if every person who follows this process gets rich, that is positive proof until someone goes through the process and fails. The theory is true until the process fails; and this process will not fail, for every person who does exactly what this book recommends will get rich.

We get rich by doing things in a Certain Way; and in order to do so, we must become able to *think* in a certain way.

Your way of doing things is the direct result of the way you think about things.

To do things in a way you want to do them, you will have to acquire the ability to think the way you want to think; this is the first step toward getting rich.

To think what you want to think is to think TRUTH, regardless of appearances.

We all have the natural and inherent power to think what we want to think, but it requires far more effort to do so than it does to think the thoughts which are suggested by appearances. To think according to appearance is easy. To think truth regardless of appearances is laborious, and requires the expenditure of more power than any other work we are called upon to perform.

There is no labor from which most people shrink as they do from that of sustained and consecutive thought; it is the hardest work in the world. This is especially true when truth is contrary to appearances. Every appearance in the visible world tends to produce a corresponding form in the mind that observes it – and this can only be prevented by holding the thought of the *truth*.

To look upon the appearance of disease will produce the form of disease in your own mind, and ultimately in your body, unless you hold the thought of the truth, which is that there is no disease; it is only an appearance, and the reality is health.

To look upon the appearances of poverty will produce corresponding forms in your own mind, unless you hold to the truth that there is no poverty; there is only abundance.

To think health when surrounded by the appearances of disease, or to think riches when in the midst of appearances of poverty, requires power. Those who acquire this power become *masterminds*, who can conquer fate and can have what they want.

This power can only be acquired by getting hold of the basic fact that is behind all appearances; and that fact is that there is one Thinking Substance, from which and by which all things are made.

Then we must grasp the truth that every thought held in this substance becomes a form, and that we can so impress our thoughts upon it as to cause them to take form and become visible things.

When we realize this, we lose all doubt and fear, for we know that we can create what we want to create; we can get what we want to have, and can become what we want to be. As a first step toward getting rich, you must believe the three fundamental statements given previously in this chapter; and in order to emphasize them. They are repeated here—

- *There is a thinking stuff from which all things are made, and which, in its original state, permeates, penetrates, and fills the interspaces of the universe.*
- *A thought, in this substance, produces the thing that is imaged by the thought.*
- *We can form things in our thought, and, by impressing our thought upon Divine substance, can cause the thing we think about to be created.*

You must lay aside all other concepts of the universe than this monistic one; and you must dwell upon this until it is fixed in your mind, and has become your habitual thought. Read these creed statements over and over again; fix every word upon your memory, and meditate upon them until you firmly believe what they say. If a doubt comes to you, cast it aside as a sin. Do not listen to arguments against this idea; do not go to places or lectures or tune in radio or television programs where a contrary concept of things is taught or preached. Do not read magazines or books which teach a different idea; if you get mixed up in your faith, all your efforts will be in vain.

Do not ask why these things are true, nor speculate as to how they can be true; simply take them on trust.

The science of getting rich begins with the absolute acceptance of this faith.

Chapter

5

INCREASING LIFE

You must get rid of the last vestige of the old idea that it is God's will that you should be poor, or it is God's purpose to keep you in poverty.

The Intelligent Substance which is God, and which is omnipresent and lives in you, is a consciously living substance. Being a consciously living substance, it must have the nature and inherent desire of every living intelligence for increase of life. Every living thing must continually seek for the enlargement of its life, because life, in the mere act of living, must increase itself.

A seed, dropped into the ground, springs into activity, and in the act of living produces a hundred more seeds; life, by living, multiplies itself. It is forever becoming more. It must do so, if it continues to be at all.

Intelligence is under this same necessity for continuous increase. Every thought we think makes it necessary for us to think another thought; consciousness is continually expanding. Every fact we learn leads us to the learning of another fact; knowledge is continually increasing. Every talent we cultivate brings to the mind the desire to cultivate another talent; we are subject to the urge of life, seeking expression, whichever drives us on to know more, to do more, and to be more.

In order to know more, do more, and be more we must have more; we must have things to use, for we learn, and do, and become, only by using things. We must get rich, so that we can live more.

The desire for riches is simply the capacity for larger life seeking fulfillment; every desire is the effort of an unexpressed possibility to come into action. It is power seeking to manifest that causes desire. That which makes you want more money is the same as that which makes the plant grow; it is *life*, seeking fuller expression.

The One Living Substance must be subject to this inherent law of all life; it is permeated with the desire to live more; that is why it is under the necessity of creating things.

The One Substance desires to live more in you; hence it wants you to have all the things you can use.

It is the desire of God that you should get rich. He wants you to get rich because He can express Himself better through you if you have plenty of things to use in giving Him expression. God can live more in you if you have unlimited command of the means of life.

The universe desires you to have everything you want to have. Nature is friendly to your plans.

Everything is naturally for you.

Make up your mind that this is true.

It is essential, however that *your purpose should harmonize with the purpose that is God's.*

You must want real life, not mere pleasure of sensual gratification. Life is the performance of function; and we really live only when we perform every function, physical, mental, and spiritual, of which we are capable, without excess in any.

You do not want to get rich in order to live swinishly, for the gratification of animal desires; that is not life. But the performance of every physical function is a part of life, and no one lives completely who denies the impulses of the body a normal and healthful expression.

You do not want to get rich solely to enjoy mental pleasures, to get knowledge, to gratify ambition, to outshine others, to be famous. All these are a legitimate part of life, but those who live for the pleasures of the intellect alone will only have a partial life, and will never be satisfied with their lot.

You do not want to get rich solely for the good of others, to lose yourself for the salvation of mankind, to experience the joys of philanthropy and sacrifice. The joys of the soul are only a part of life; and they are no better or nobler than any other part.

You want to get rich in order that you may eat, drink, and be merry when it is time to do these things. You want to get rich so you may surround yourself with beautiful things, see distant lands, feed your mind, and develop your intellect. You want to get rich in order that you may love others and do kind things, and be able to play a good part in helping the world to find truth.

But remember that *extreme* altruism is no better and no nobler than extreme selfishness; both are mistakes.

Get rid of the idea that God wants you to sacrifice yourself for others, and that you can secure his favor by doing so; God requires nothing of the kind.

What God wants is that you should make the most of yourself, for yourself. *You can help others more by making the most of yourself than in any other way.*

You can make the most of yourself only by getting rich; so it is right and praiseworthy that you should give your first and best thought to the work of acquiring wealth.

Remember, however, that the desire of Substance is for all, and its movements must be for more life to all. It cannot be made to work for less life to any, because it is equally in all, seeking riches and life.

Intelligent Substance will make things for you, but it will not take things away from someone else and give them to you.

You must get rid of the thought of competition. You are to create, not to compete for what is already created.

You do not have to take anything away from anyone. You do not have to drive sharp bargains.

You do not have to cheat, or to take advantage. You do not need to pay your workers less than they deserve.

You do not have to covet the property of others, or to look at it with wishful eyes. You can have anything you like without taking it away from others.

You are to become a *creator*, not a competitor. You are going to get what you want, but in such a way that when you get it every other person will gain as well.

Do not become greedy. Sure, greedy people may become millionaires, but they will always be wretched and mean and will even consider themselves outwardly poor so long as there is a person in the world who is richer than they are.

If you would realize true prosperity, do not settle down as many have done, into the belief that if you do right everything will go wrong. Do not let the word 'competition' shake your faith in the supremacy of righteousness.

Under all circumstances *do that which you believe to be right* and trust the Law; trust the Divine Power that is imminent in the universe, and it will never desert you. You will always be protected. By such a trust, all your losses will be converted into gain, and all curses that threaten you will be transmuted into blessings. Never let go of integrity, generosity, and love, for all these, coupled with energy, will lift you into the truly prosperous state. Do not believe the world when it tells you that you must always attend to 'number one' first and to others afterwards. To do this is not to think of others at all, but only of one's own comforts. To those who practice this the day will come when all will desert them, and when they cry out in their loneliness and anguish there will be no one to hear and help them.

To consider one's self before all others is to cramp and warp and hinder every noble and divine impulse. Let your soul expand. Let your heart reach out to others in loving and generous warmth, and great and lasting will be your joy, and all prosperity will come to you.

A woman who had a great love for poultry decided that she would go into the chicken business, so she rented a small piece of land and gave up her time to the production of the finest possible breed of hens. During her years with the fowls she gained a great deal of practical, even metaphysical knowledge.

In relating some of her many observations and experiences she said: "Chickens are just like human beings, they have the same desires and they make the same mistakes and suffer from the reaction of their ignorance just as we do. I never feed the chickens, but I find something to use as a lesson for myself.

"Whenever it is time to feed them I take a huge pan full of many good things which chickens like and, placing it in the center of the yard, call them. Some of them are near, some of them are far away, but at the sound of my voice and call, they all come running pell-mell. Some of the hens that are nearest the pan grab a mouthful out of it and run away toward the corner of the yard. Others, seeing them with a piece of food in their mouths, chase wildly after them, totally ignoring my call and the full pan of food just before them.

"Before many minutes all the hens are out in the farthest corners, away from the food, fighting, scrambling and tumbling over each other in their attempts to secure the morsel which was in the mouths of the few, entirely unconscious of the big full pan of supply waiting just within easy reach.

"Isn't this the way with humans? Someone gets a little supply out of the great universal pan and then the blind beside them begin to struggle with them to get possession of their little bit without going straight to the universal source itself which is always waiting, full and free for them to come and take. The universal good awaits our return with the same natural law that awaited the hens.

"When the hens got through struggling and no one had anything, the pan was still standing waiting to supply in full, the hunger and wants of those who found their way back. I have to call them back many times before they satisfy themselves from the pan and not from the bits they wrested from each other."

There are some people who have become very rich, sometimes purely by their extraordinary ability on the plane of competition; and sometimes they unconsciously relate themselves to Substance in its great purposes and movements for the general good through industrial evolution. Such nineteenth century moguls as Rockefeller, Carnegie, Morgan, Edison and others contributed much to welfare of the country by creating opportunities for countless workers and shareholders. In the early twentieth century, manufacturing geniuses such as Henry Ford, Harvey Firestone, and David Sarnoff, by systematizing and organizing productive industries contributed immensely toward increased life for all.

The Henry Ford of the late 20th century was Bill Gates. Just as Ford revolutionized the transportation industry by creating an automobile that most anyone could afford and drive, Bill gates revolutionized the computer industry by designing software that enabled everybody – not just the specialized technocrats – to be able to use computers, and later making the Personal Computer a virtual necessity in every office, school, and most homes. This resulted in Bill Gates accruing billions of dollars and becoming the richest man in America.

He first became entranced with computers and began programming them at age 13. In 1973, he entered Harvard University as a freshman, where he lived down the hall from Steve Ballmer, now Microsoft's chief executive officer. While at Harvard, Gates developed a version of the programming language BASIC for the first microcomputer.

By the time he reached his junior year, Gates was so absorbed in his dream of building a software company that he left Harvard to devote his energies to fulfilling this dream. A few years earlier, he and his childhood friend Paul Allen had formed a company, Microsoft, as the vehicle for this endeavor. Guided by a belief that the computer would be a valuable tool on every office desktop and in every home, they began developing software for personal computers. Gates' foresight and his vision for personal computing have been central to the success of Microsoft and the software industry.

Having achieved his major goal, Bill Gates continues to pursue new goals both in the business of creating ever-improving computer programs and in his philanthropic work, having founded with his wife, Melinda, the largest charitable foundation in the world.

Ray Kroc is a good example of another person who made his dream come true. Kroc was a salesman of milkshake mixers. Most of his customers – restaurants and diners – purchased one or two units. When he received an order for eight mixers from a small food outlet in San Bernardino, California, he decided to visit them and see how they could sell so many shakes. It was the busiest restaurant he had ever seen. The brothers offered a very limited menu: hamburgers, cheeseburgers, French fries, shakes and soft drinks – all at the lowest prices in the area.

Kroc saw an opportunity. If he could open a chain of these restaurants, each as productive and profitable as this, money would flow in. He proposed the idea to the McDonald brothers and agreed to implement it. Within a few years, McDonald's became the top-selling food outlet in the country, and became the prototype of the fast-food industry. Kroc later bought out the McDonald brothers and expanded the business into an international phenomenon and making him one of the richest men of his time.

Many men and women recognized the opportunities created by these creative giants and using their own initiative and capitalizing on their individual talents, developed businesses which not only made them rich, but opened the door to riches for still more people.

Riches secured by destructive competition are never satisfactory and permanent; they are yours today, and another's tomorrow. Remember, if you are to become rich in a scientific and certain way, you must rise entirely out of the competitive thought. You must never think for a moment that the supply is limited.

Know that there are countless millions of dollars' worth of treasure in the mountains of the earth, not yet brought to light; and know that if there were not, more would be created from Thinking Substance to supply your needs.

Know that the money you need will come, even if it is necessary for a thousand people to be led to the discovery of new resources tomorrow.

Never look at the visible supply; look always at the limitless riches in Divine Substance, and *know* that they are coming to you as fast as you can receive and use them. Nobody, by cornering the visible supply, can prevent you from getting what is yours.

So never allow yourself to think for an instant that all the best building spots will be taken before you get ready to build your house, unless you hurry. Never worry about the conglomerates and cartels, and get anxious for fear they will soon come to own the whole earth. Never get afraid that you will lose what you want because some other person 'beats you to it.' That cannot possibly happen; you are not seeking anything that is possessed by anybody else; you are causing what you want to be created from Divine Substance, and the supply is without limits. Stick to the formulated statement:

- *There is a thinking stuff from which all things are made, and which, in its original state, permeates, penetrates, and fills the interspaces of the universe.*
- *A thought, in this substance, produces the thing that is imaged by the thought.*
- *We can form things in his thought, and, by impressing our thought upon Divine substance, can cause the thing we think about to be created.*

Chapter

6

HOW RICHES COME TO YOU

Some people say that you do not have to drive sharp bargains. That does not mean that you do not have to drive any bargains at all, or that you are above the necessity for having any dealings with others. It means that you will not need to deal with them unfairly. You do not have to get something for nothing, *but can give to all others more than you take from them.*

You cannot give others more in cash market value than you take from them, but you can give them more in use value than the cash value of the thing you take from them. The paper, ink, and other material in this book may not be worth the money you pay for it; but if the ideas suggested by it bring you thousands of dollars, you have not been wronged by those who sold it to you. They have given you a great use value for a small cash value.

Let us suppose that you own a picture by one of the great artists, which, in any civilized community, is worth thousands of dollars. You take it to Baffin Bay, and by 'salesmanship' induce an Eskimo to give a bundle of furs worth $500 for it. You have really wronged him, for he has no use for the picture; it has no use value to him; it will not add to his life.

But suppose you give him a gun worth $50 for his furs; then he has made a good bargain. He has use for the gun; it will get him many more furs and much food; it will add to his life in every way; it will make him rich.

When you rise from the competitive to the creative plane, you can scan your business transactions very strictly, and if you are selling anything that does not add more to the life of the buyer than the thing you get in exchange, you can afford to stop it. You do not have to beat anybody in business. And if you are in a business that does beat people, get out of it at once.

Give people more in use value than you take from them in cash value; then you are adding to the life of the world by every business transaction.

If you have people working for you, you must take from them more in cash value than you pay them in wages. You can so organize your business that it will be filled with the principle of advancement, and so that each employee who wishes to do so may advance a little every day.

You can make your business do for your employees what this book is doing for you. You can so conduct your business that it will be a sort of ladder, by which all employees will be given the opportunity to move ahead, and if they take the trouble may themselves climb to riches And finally, because you are to cause the creation of your riches from Divine Substance which permeates all your environment, it does not follow that they are to take shape from the atmosphere and come into being before your eyes.

If you want a computer, for instance, this does not mean that you are to impress the thought of a computer on Thinking Substance until the machine is formed without hands, in the room where you sit, or elsewhere. But if you want a computer, hold the mental image of it with the most positive certainty that it is being made, or is on its way to you. After once forming the thought, have the most absolute and unquestioning faith that the computer is coming; never think of it, or speak, of it, in any other way than as being sure to arrive. Claim it as already yours.

It will be brought to you by the power of the Supreme Intelligence, acting upon your mind. If you live in Maine, it may be that somebody will arrive from Texas or Japan to engage in some transaction that will result in your getting what you want.

If so, the whole matter will be as much to that person's advantage as it is to yours.

Do not forget for a moment that the Thinking Substance is through all, in all, communicating with all, and can influence all. The desire of Thinking Substance for fuller life and better living has caused the creation of all the computers already made; and it can cause the creation of millions more, and will, whenever people set it in motion by desire and faith, and by acting in a Certain Way.

You can certainly have a computer in your house; and it is just as certain that you can have any other thing or things which you want, and which you will use for the advancement of your own life and the lives of others.

Divine Substance wants to live all that is possible in you, and wants you to have all that you can or will use for the living of the most abundant life.

If you fix upon your consciousness the fact that the desire you feel for the possession of riches is one with the desire of Omnipotence for more complete expression, your faith becomes invincible.

A little girl was sitting at a piano, and vainly trying to bring harmony out of the keys. She was grieved and provoked by her inability to play real music. She was asked the cause of her vexation, and she answered, "I can feel the music in me, but I can't make my hands go right." The music in her was the Urge of Divine Substance, containing all the possibilities of all life; all that there is of music was seeking expression through the child.

God, the One Substance, is trying to live and do and enjoy things through humanity. He is saying, "I want hands to build wonderful structures, to play divine harmonies, to paint glorious pictures; I want feet to run my errands, eyes to see my beauties, tongues to tell mighty truths and to sing marvelous songs," and so on.

All that there is of possibility is seeking expression through humankind. God wants those who can play music to have pianos and every other instrument, and to have the means to cultivate their talents to the fullest extent. He wants those who can appreciate beauty to be able to surround themselves with beautiful things. He wants those who can discern truth to have every opportunity to travel and observe. He wants those who can appreciate dress to be beautifully clothed, and those who can appreciate good food to be luxuriously fed.

God wants all these things because it is Himself that enjoys and appreciates them.

It is God who wants to play, and sing, and enjoy beauty, and proclaim truth and wear fine clothes, and eat good foods.

The desire you feel for riches is God, seeking to express Himself in you as He sought to find expression in the little girl at the piano.

So you need not hesitate to ask largely. Your part is to focus and express the desire to God.

This is a difficult point with most people. They retain something of the old idea that poverty and self-sacrifice are pleasing to God. They look upon poverty as a part of the plan, a necessity of nature. They have the idea that God has finished His work, and made all that He can make, and that the majority of people must stay poor because there is not enough to go around. They hold to so much of this erroneous thought that they feel ashamed to ask for wealth. They try not to want more than a very modest competence, just enough to make them fairly comfortable.

There is the case of the student who was told that he must get in mind a clear picture of the things he desired, so that the creative thought of them might be impressed on Divine Substance. He was a very poor man, living in a rented house, and having only what he earned from day to day. He could not grasp the fact that all wealth was his. So, after thinking the matter over, he decided that he might reasonably ask for a new rug for the floor of his best room, and a stove to heat the house during the cold weather.

Following the instructions given in this book, he obtained these things in a few months. Then it dawned upon him that he had not asked enough. He went through the house, in which he lived, and planned all the improvements he would like to make in it. He mentally added a bay window here and a room there, until it was complete in his mind as his ideal home; and then he planned its furnishings.

Holding the whole picture in his mind, he began living in the Certain Way, and moving toward what he wanted. Now he owns the house and is rebuilding it after the form of his mental image. And with still larger faith, he is going on to get greater things. It has been unto him according to his faith, and it is so with you and with all of us.

Chapter

7

GRATITUDE

The illustrations given in the last chapter will have conveyed to the reader the fact that the first step toward getting rich is to convey the idea of your wants to the Divine Substance.

This is true, and you will see that in order to do so it becomes necessary to relate yourself to the Divine Intelligence in a harmonious way.

The whole process of mental adjustment and atonement can be summed up in one word, *gratitude*.

First, you believe that there is one Intelligent Substance, from which all things proceed; second, you believe that this Substance gives you everything you desire; and third, you relate yourself to it by a feeling of deep and profound gratitude.

Many people who order their lives rightly in all other ways are kept in poverty by their lack of gratitude. Having received one gift from God, they cut the wires that connect them with Him by failing to make acknowledgment.

It is easy to understand that the nearer we live to the source of wealth, the more wealth we shall receive. It is also easy to understand that the soul that is always grateful lives in closer touch with God than the one that never looks to Him in thankful acknowledgment.

The more gratefully we fix our minds on the Supreme when good things come to us, the more good things we will receive, and the more rapidly they will come. The reason simply is that the mental attitude of gratitude draws the mind into closer touch with the source from which the blessings come.

If it is a new thought to you that gratitude brings your whole mind into closer harmony with the creative energies of the universe, consider it well, and you will see that it is true. The good things you already possess have come to you along the line of obedience to certain laws. Gratitude will lead your mind out along the ways by which things come; and it will keep you in close harmony with creative thought and prevent you from falling into competitive thought.

Gratitude alone can keep you looking toward the All, and prevent you from falling into the error of thinking of the supply as limited; and to do that would be fatal to your hopes.

There is a Law of Gratitude, and it is absolutely necessary that you should observe the law, if you are to get the results you seek.

The law of gratitude is the natural principle that action and reaction are always equal, and in opposite directions.

The grateful outreaching of your mind in thankful praise to the Supreme is a liberation or expenditure of force. It cannot fail to reach that to which it addressed, and the reaction is an instantaneous movement toward you.

'Draw nigh unto God, and He will draw nigh unto you.' That is a statement of psychological truth.

And if your gratitude is strong and constant, the reaction in Divine Substance will be strong and continuous; the movement of the things you want will be always toward you. You cannot exercise much power without gratitude; for it is gratitude that keeps you connected with Power.

But the value of gratitude does not consist solely in getting you more blessings in the future. Without gratitude you cannot long keep from dissatisfied thought regarding things as they are.

The moment you permit your mind to dwell with dissatisfaction upon things as they are, you begin to lose ground. You fix attention upon the common, the ordinary, the poor, and the squalid and mean; and your mind takes the form of these things. Then you will transmit these forms or mental images to the Divine, and the common, the poor, the squalid, and mean will come to you.

To permit your mind to dwell upon the inferior is to become inferior and to surround yourself with inferior things.

On the other hand, to fix your attention on the best is to surround yourself with the best, and to become the best.

The Creative Power within us makes us into the image of that to which we give our attention.

We are Thinking Substance, and thinking substance always takes the form of that which it thinks about.

The grateful mind is constantly fixed upon the best; therefore it tends to become the best; it takes the form or character of the best, and will receive the best.

Also, faith is born of gratitude. The grateful mind continually expects good things, and expectation becomes faith. The reaction of gratitude upon one's own mind produces faith; and every outgoing wave of grateful thanksgiving increases faith. If you have no feeling of gratitude, you cannot long retain a living faith; and without a living faith you cannot get rich by the creative method, as we shall see in the following chapters.

It is necessary, then, to cultivate the habit of being grateful for every good thing that comes to you and to give thanks continuously.

And because all things have contributed to your advancement, you should include all things in your gratitude.

Do not waste time thinking or talking about the shortcomings or wrong actions of plutocrats or corporate giants. Their organization of the world has made your opportunity; all you get really comes to you because of them.

Do not rage against, corrupt politicians; if it were not for politicians we should fall into anarchy, and your opportunity would be greatly lessened.

God has worked a long time and very patiently to bring us up to where we are in industry and government, and He is going right on with His work. There is not the least doubt that He will do away with plutocrats, captains of industry, and politicians as soon as they can be spared; but in the meantime, behold they are all very good. Remember that they are all helping to arrange the lines of transmission along which your riches will come to you, and be grateful to them all. This will bring you into harmonious relations with the good in everything, and the good in everything will move toward you.

Chapter

8

THINKING IN THE CERTAIN WAY

Turn back to chapter 6 and read again the story of the man who formed a mental image of his house, and you will get a fair idea of the initial step toward getting rich. You must form a clear and definite mental picture of what you want; you cannot transmit an idea unless you have it yourself.

You must have it before you can give it; and many people fail to impress Thinking Substance because they have themselves only a vague and misty concept of the things they want to do, to have, or to become.

It is not enough that you should have a general desire for wealth 'to do good with'; everybody has that desire.

It is not enough that you should have a wish to travel, see things, live more, and enjoy life. Everybody has those desires also. If you were going to send a message to a friend, you would not send the letters of the alphabet in their order, and let your friend construct the message for him or herself; nor would you take words at random from the dictionary. You would send a coherent sentence; one which meant something. When you try to impress your wants upon Substance, remember that it must be done by a coherent statement; you must know what you want, and be definite. You can never get rich, or start the creative power into action, by sending out unformed longings and vague desires.

Go over your desires just as that man went over his house; see just what you want, and get a clear mental picture of it as you wish it to look when you get it.

That clear mental picture you must have continually in mind, as the sailor has in mind the port toward which the ship is sailing; you must keep your face toward it all the time. You must no more lose sight of it than the steersman loses sight of the compass.

It is not necessary to take exercises in concentration, or to set apart special times for prayer and affirmation, or to 'go into the silence,' or to do occult stunts of any kind. These things are well enough, but all you need is to know what you want, and to want it badly enough so that it will stay in your thoughts.

Spend as much of your leisure time as you can in contemplating your picture, but it is not necessary to take exercises to concentrate your mind on a thing that you really want. However, it requires real effort to fix your attention upon the things you do not really care about.

Unless your desire to get rich is strong enough to hold your thoughts directed to the purpose it will hardly be worthwhile for you to try to carry out the instructions given in this book.

The methods set forth are for people whose desire for riches is strong enough to overcome mental laziness and the love of ease, and make them work.

The more clear and definite you make your picture then, and the more you dwell upon it, bringing out all its delightful details, the stronger your desire will be. The stronger your desire, the easier it will be to hold your mind fixed upon the picture of what you want.

Engage your subconscious mind. Keep saying, "I am prospering every day." "I am growing in wealth and in wisdom every day." "Every day my wealth is multiplying." "I am advancing, growing, and moving forward financially." Our subconscious mind accepts our beliefs, feeling, convictions and what we consciously accept as true.

Something more is necessary, however, than merely to see the picture clearly. If that is all you do, you are only a dreamer, and will have little or no power for accomplishment.

Behind your clear vision must be the purpose to realize it – to bring it out in tangible expression.

And behind this purpose must be an invincible and unwavering *faith* that the thing is already yours; that it is 'at hand' and you have only to take possession of it.

Live in the new house, mentally, until it takes form around you physically. In the mental realm, enter at once into full enjoyment of the things you want.

See the things you want as if they were actually around you all the time; see yourself as owning and using them. Make use of them in imagination just as you will use them when they are your tangible possessions. Dwell upon your mental picture until it is clear and distinct, and then take the Mental Attitude of Ownership toward everything in that picture. Take possession of it, in mind, in the full faith that it is actually yours. Hold to this mental ownership; do not waiver for an instant in the faith that it is real.

The story is told of John W. Gates and his perfect manifestation of this principle. He came to San Antonio as the agent of a barbed wire company, and saw the great possibilities in Texas. He expressed his belief to an old resident of San Antonio This old citizen was complaining that he could only just make a living here. "Make a living!" said Gates. "Any man can get rich here in ten years." "Well," said the old citizen, "I've been here more than ten years and I have not got rich." "Perhaps not," remarked Gates, "wealth does not hunt one up and spring from some unseen angle. One has to keep constantly on the trail, and since there are so many trails leading in the right direction in Texas, if you will keep an eye on me I'll show you how the trick is turned."

Some years later when Gates became heavily interested in the lumber business in the eastern part of the state, someone said to him: "You cannot make the lumber business go here, since there is no means of shipping it."

"Never mind," remarked Gates, "I'll make a place to ship it from and then I'll show you that there is enough lumber in Texas to weatherboard the universe."

Sometime after this he met the old man to whom he had talked about getting rich when he first came to Texas. "I hear you are making it go," said the old man, "and that you are really getting rich, as you said you would."

"Making it go," remarked the man who saw possibilities. "Damn it! Things are making me go. Things come so easily here that I am constantly on the dodge to keep from owning the whole state of Texas. It's the easiest game I ever played. No odds what kind of a hand you have, if you bet enough you'll win."

There are thousands of failures simply because they did not have the genius to see an opportunity, but there are more failures because when opportunity was everywhere they lacked the thought force necessary to push it into form. This is not just the same as the laws of 'mind your own business.'

And remember what was said in a proceeding chapter about gratitude; be as thankful for it all the time as you expect to be when it has taken form. If you can sincerely thank God for the things, which as yet you own only in imagination, you have real faith. You will get rich. You will cause the creation of whatsoever you want.

You do not need to pray repeatedly for things you want; it is not necessary to tell God about it every day.

Your part is to intelligently formulate your desire for the things which make for a larger life, and to get these desire arranged into a coherent whole. Then you must impress this Whole Desire upon the Divine Substance, which has the power and the will to bring you what you want.

You do not make this impression by repeating strings of words. You make it by holding the vision with unshakable *purpose* to attain it, and with steadfast *faith* that you do attain it.

The answer to prayer is not according to your faith while you are talking, but according to your faith while you are working.

You cannot impress the mind of God by having a special Sabbath day set apart to tell Him what you want, and then forgetting Him during the rest of the week. You cannot impress Him by having special hours to go into your closet and pray, if you then dismiss the matter from your mind until the hour of prayer comes again.

Oral prayer is well enough, and has its effect, especially upon yourself, in clarifying your vision and strengthening your faith; but it is not your oral petitions that get you what you want. In order to get rich you do not need a 'sweet hour of prayer,' you need to 'pray without ceasing.' Prayer means holding steadily to your vision, with the purpose to cause its creation into solid form, and the faith that you are doing so.

The whole matter turns on receiving, once you have clearly formed your vision. When you have formed it, it is well to make an oral statement, addressing the Supreme in reverent prayer; and from that moment you must, in mind, receive what you ask for. Live in the new house; wear the fine clothes; ride in the automobile; go on the journey, and confidently plan for greater journeys. Think and speak of all the things you have asked for in terms of actual present ownership. Imagine an environment, and a financial condition exactly as you want them, and live all the time in that imaginary environment and financial condition. Mind, however, that you do not do this as a mere dreamer and castle builder. Hold to the *faith* that the imaginary is being realized, and to the *purpose* to realize it. Remember that it is faith and purpose in the use of the imagination, which make the difference between the scientist and the dreamer. And having learned this fact, it is here that you must learn the proper use of the Will.

Sir John Templeton is a very religious man who not only observes his religion on the Sabbath but also incorporates it in all of his business activities.

Templeton was better than most people at investing money because people often made investments based on emotion and ignorance and not common sense. He felt that by using his skill in investing, he could not only provide a needed service to the small investor, but make a good deal of money for himself.

To accomplish this he started a group of mutual funds to manage other people's money. This was a pioneering project as at that time mutual funds were a relatively new concept. Templeton honed that concept into one of the most important investment concepts existing today.

He reminisced that at the Templeton Growth Fund's first annual meeting, the participants consisted of John Templeton, one part-time employee and one shareholder. "We held the meeting in the dining room of a retired General Foods executive, to save money."

The Templeton funds now have more than 600 employees worldwide and $36 billion in assets. Driving that growth is the Templeton Group's well-earned reputation as the premier fund group for investing. A $10,000 investment in The Templeton Growth Fund 40 years ago is worth $3 million today.

By the time he retired and sold his Templeton Group fund interests in 1992 (estimated at $400 million), in addition to his own success, he had helped, he estimates, a million people make money.

Chapter

9

HOW TO USE THE WILL

To set about getting rich in a scientific way, you do not try to apply your will power to anything outside of yourself.

You have no right to do so, anyway.

It is wrong to apply your will to other men and women, in order to get them to do what you wish done.

It is as flagrantly wrong to coerce people by mental power, as it is to coerce them by physical power. If compelling people by physical force to do things for you reduces them to slavery, compelling them by mental means accomplishes exactly the same thing; the only difference is in methods. If taking things from people by physical force is robbery, then taking things by mental force is robbery also; there is no difference in principle.

You have no right to use your will power upon another person, even 'for his or her own good' for you do not know what is for that person's good. The secret of getting rich does not require you to apply power or force to any other person, in any way whatsoever. There is not the slightest necessity for doing so; indeed, any attempt to use your will upon others will only tend to defeat your purpose.

You do not need to apply your will to things, in order to compel them to come to you.

That would simply be trying to coerce God, and would be foolish and useless, as well as irreverent.

You do not have to compel God to give you good things, any more than you have to use your will power to make the sun rise.

You do not have to use your will power to conquer an unfriendly deity or to make stubborn and rebellious forces do your bidding.

Substance is friendly to you, and is more anxious to give you what you want than you are to get it.

To get rich, you need only to use your will power upon yourself.

When you know what to think and do, then you must use your will to compel yourself to think and do the right things. That is the legitimate use of the will in getting what you want – to use it in holding yourself to the right course. Use your will to keep yourself thinking and acting in the Certain Way.

Do not try to project your will, or your thoughts, or your mind out into space, to 'act' on things or people.

Keep your mind at home; it can accomplish more there than elsewhere.

Use your mind to form a mental image of what you want, and to hold that vision with faith and purpose; and use your will to keep your mind working in the Right Way.

The more steady and continuous your faith and purpose, the more rapidly you will get rich, because you will make only *positive* impressions upon Substance; and you will not neutralize or offset them by negative impressions.

The picture of your desires, held with faith and purpose, is taken up by the Divine, and permeates it to great distances throughout the universe.

As this impression spreads, all things are set moving toward its realization; every living thing, every inanimate thing, and the things yet uncreated, are stirred toward bringing into being that which you want. All force begins to be exerted in that direction; all things begin to move toward you. The minds of people, everywhere, are influenced toward doing the things necessary to the fulfilling of your desires; and they work for you, unconsciously.

But you can check all this by starting a negative impression in the Divine Substance. Doubt or unbelief is as certain to start a movement away from you, as faith and purpose are to start one toward you. It is by not understanding this that most people who try to make use of 'mental science' in getting rich make their failure. Every hour and moment you spend in giving heed to doubts and fears, every hour you spend in worry, every hour in which your soul is possessed by unbelief, sets a current away from you in the whole domain of intelligent Substance. All the promises are unto them that believe, and unto them only.

Since belief is all-important, it behooves you to guard your thoughts. As your beliefs will be shaped to a very great extent by the things you observe and think about, it is important that you should command your attention.

And here the will comes into use; for it is by your will that you determine upon what things your attention shall be fixed.

If you want to become rich, you must not make a study of poverty.

Things are not brought into being by thinking about their opposites. Health is never to be attained by studying disease and thinking about disease; righteousness is not to be promoted by studying sin and thinking about sin; and no one ever got rich by studying poverty and thinking about poverty.

Medicine as a science of disease has increased disease; religion as a science of sin has promoted sin, and economics as a study of poverty will fill the world with wretchedness and want.

Do not talk about poverty; do not investigate it, or concern yourself with it. Never mind what its causes are; you have nothing to do with them.

What concerns you is the cure.

Get rich! That is the best way you can help the poor.

If you fill your mind with pictures of poverty, you cannot hold the mental image that is to make you rich. Do not read books or papers that give circumstantial accounts of the wretchedness of the tenement dwellers, of the horrors of child labor, and so on. Do not read anything that fills your mind with gloomy images of want and suffering.

You cannot help the poor in the least by knowing about these things; and the widespread knowledge of them does not tend at all to do away with poverty. What tends to do away with poverty is not the getting of pictures of poverty into your mind, but getting pictures of wealth into the minds of the poor. You are not deserting the poor in their misery when you refuse to allow your mind to be filled with pictures of that misery.

Poverty can be done away with, not by increasing the number of well to do people who think about poverty, but by increasing the number of poor people who purpose with faith to get rich.

The poor do not need charity; they need inspiration. Charity only sends them a loaf of bread to keep them alive in their wretchedness, or gives them an entertainment to make them forget for an hour or two; but inspiration will cause them to rise out of their misery. If you want to help the poor, demonstrate to them that they can become rich; prove it by getting rich yourself.

The only way in which poverty will ever be banished from this world is by getting a large and constantly increasing number of people to practice the teachings of this book.

People must be taught to become rich by creation, not by competition. Those who become rich by competition throw down behind them the ladder by which they rise, and keep others down; but those who get rich by creation open a way for thousands to follow them and inspire them to do so.

You are not showing hardness of heart or an unfeeling disposition when you refuse to pity poverty, see poverty, read about poverty, or think or talk about it, or to listen to those who do talk about it. Use your will power to keep your mind *off* the subject of poverty, and to keep it fixed with faith and purpose *on* the vision of what you want.

Chapter

10

FURTHER USE OF THE WILL

You cannot retain a true and clear vision of wealth if you are constantly turning our attention to opposing pictures, whether they are external or imaginary.

Do not tell of your past troubles of a financial nature, if you have had them, do not think of them at all. Do not tell of the poverty of your parents or the hardships of your early life. To do any of these things is to mentally class yourself with the poor for the time being, and it will certainly check the movement of things in your direction.

'Let the dead bury their dead.'

Put poverty and all things that pertain to poverty completely behind you.

You have accepted a certain theory of the universe as being correct, and are resting all your hopes of happiness on its being correct. What can you gain by giving heed to conflicting theories?

Do not read books that tell you that the world is soon coming to an end; and do not read the writing of pessimistic philosophers who tell you that it is going to the devil.

The world is not going to the devil; it is going to God. It is wonderful becoming.

True, there may be a good many things in existing conditions that are disagreeable; but what is the use of studying them when they are certainly passing away, and when the study of them only tends to check their passing and keep them with us? Why give time and attention to things that are being removed by evolutionary growth, when you can hasten their removal only by promoting the evolutionary growth as far as your part of it goes?

No matter how horrible in seeming may be the conditions in certain countries, sections, or places, you waste your time and destroy your own chances by considering them.

You should interest yourself in the world's becoming rich.

Think of the riches the world is coming into, instead of the poverty it is growing out of. Bear in mind that the only way in which you can assist the world in growing rich is by growing rich yourself through the creative method – not the competitive one.

Give your attention wholly to riches; ignore poverty.

Whenever you think or speak of those who are poor, think and speak of them as those who are becoming rich as those who are to be congratulated rather than pitied. Then they and others will catch the inspiration, and begin to search for the way out.

Because you give your whole time and mind and thought to riches, it does not follow that you are to be sordid or mean.

To become really rich is the noblest aim you can have in life, for it includes everything else.

On the competitive plane, the struggle to get rich is a godless scramble for power over others; but when we come into the creative mind, all this is changed.

All that is possible in the way of greatness and development of your soul, of service and lofty endeavor comes by way of getting rich; all is made possible by the use of things.

If you lack for physical health, you will find that the attainment of it is conditional on your getting rich.

Only those who are emancipated from financial worry, and who have the means to live a carefree existence and follow hygienic practices can have and retain health.

Moral and spiritual greatness is possible only to those who are above the competitive battle for existence. Only those who are becoming rich on the plane of creative thought are free from the degrading influences of competition. If your heart is set on domestic happiness, remember that love flourishes best where there is refinement, a high level of thought, and freedom from corrupting influences; and these are to be found only where riches are attained by the exercise of creative thought, without strife or rivalry.

You can aim at nothing so great or noble as to become rich; and you must fix your attention upon your mental picture of riches, to the exclusion of all that may tend to dim or obscure the vision.

You must learn to see the underlying *truth* in all things. You must see beneath all seemingly wrong conditions that life is ever moving forward toward fuller expression and more complete happiness.

It is the truth that there is no such thing as poverty – that there is only wealth.

Some people remain in poverty because they are ignorant of the fact that there is wealth for them. These people can best be taught by showing them the way to affluence in your own person and practice.

Others are poor because, while they feel that there is a way out, they are too intellectually indolent to put forth the mental effort necessary to find that way and by travel it. For these the very best thing you can do is to arouse their desire and by showing them the happiness that comes from being rightly rich.

Others still are poor because, while they have some notion of science, they have become so swamped and lost in the maze of metaphysical and occult theories that they do not know which road to take. They try a mixture of many systems and fail in all. For these, again, the very best thing to do is to show the right way in your own person and practice. An ounce of doing things is worth a pound of theorizing.

The very best thing you can do for the whole world is to make the most of yourself.

You can serve God and humankind in no more effective way than by getting rich; that is, if you get rich by the creative method and not by the competitive one.

Read this book every day. Keep it with you. Commit it to memory. Do not think about other 'systems' and theories. If you do, you will begin to have doubts and to be uncertain and wavering in your thought; and then you will begin to make failures.

After you have made good and become rich, you may study other systems as much as you please; but until you are quite sure that you have gained what you want, do not read anything on this line but this book.

And read only the most optimistic comments on the world's news – those in harmony with your picture.

This and the preceding chapters have brought us to the following statement of basic facts—

- *There is a thinking stuff from which all things are made, and which, in its original state, permeates, penetrates, and fills the interspaces of the universe.*
- *A thought, in this substance, produces the thing that is imaged by the thought.*
- *We can form things in our thought, and, by impressing our thought upon Divine substance, can cause the thing we think about to be created.*
- *In order to do this, we must pass from the competitive to the creative mind. We must form a clear mental picture of the things we want, and hold this picture in our thoughts with the fixed* purpose *to get what we want, and the unwavering* faith *that we do get what we want, closing our mind against all that may tend to shake our purpose, dim our vision, or quench our faith.*

And in addition to all this, we shall now see that he must live and act in a Certain Way.

Chapter
11

ACTING IN THE CERTAIN WAY

Thought is the creative power, or the impelling force that causes the creative power to act. Thinking in a Certain Way will bring riches to you, but you must not rely upon thought alone, paying no attention to personal action. That is the rock upon which many otherwise scientific metaphysical thinkers meet shipwreck – the failure to connect thought with personal action.

We have not yet reached the stage of development, even supposing such a stage to be possible, in which we can create directly from Divine Substance without nature's processes or the work of human hands. We must not only think, but our personal action must supplement our thought.

By thought you can cause the gold in the hearts of the mountains to be impelled toward you, but it will not mine itself, refine itself, coin itself into double eagles, and come rolling along the roads seeking its way into your pocket.

Under the impelling power of the Supreme Spirit, your affairs will be so ordered that someone will be led to mine the gold for you. Other people's business transactions will be so directed that the gold will be brought toward you, and you must so arrange your own business affairs that you may be able to receive it when it comes to you. Your thought makes all things, animate and inanimate, work to bring you what you want. However, your personal activity must be such that you can rightly receive what you want when it reaches you. You are not to take it as charity, nor to steal it. You must give others more in use value than they give you in cash value.

The scientific use of thought consists in forming a clear and distinct mental image of what you want by holding fast to the purpose to get what you want, and in realizing with grateful faith that you do get what you want.

Do not try to 'project' your thought in any mysterious or occult way, with the idea of having it go out and do things for you. That is wasted effort, and will weaken your power to think with sanity.

The action of thought in getting rich is fully explained in the preceding chapters. Your faith and purpose positively impress your vision upon Divine Substance, which has *the same desire for more life that you have*; and this vision, received from you, sets all the creative forces at work *in and through their regular channels of action*, but directed toward you.

It is not your part to guide or supervise the creative process. All you have to do with that is to retain your vision, stick to your purpose, and maintain your faith and gratitude.

But you must act in a Certain Way, so that you can appropriate what is yours when it comes to you; so that you can meet the things you have in your picture, and put them in their proper places as they arrive.

You can really see the truth of this. When things reach you, they will be in the hands of other people, who will ask an equivalent for them.

And you can only get what is yours by giving others what is theirs.

Your pocketbook is not going to be transformed into a magic purse, which shall be always full of money without effort on your part.

This is the crucial point in the science of getting rich – right here, where thought and personal action must be combined. There are very many people who, consciously or unconsciously, set the creative forces in action by the strength and persistence of their desires, but who remain poor because they do not provide for the reception of the thing they want when it comes.

By thought, the thing you want is brought to you; by action you receive it.

Whatever your action is to be, it is evident that you must act *now*. You cannot act in the past, and it is essential to the clearness of your mental vision that you dismiss the past from your mind. You cannot act in the future, for the future is not here yet. And you cannot tell how you will want to act in any future contingency until that contingency has arrived.

Because you are not in the right business or the right environment now, do not think that you must postpone action until you get into the right business or environment. And do not spend time in the present taking thought as to the best course in possible future emergencies. Have faith in your ability to meet any emergency when it arrives.

If you act in the present with your mind on the future, your present action will be with a divided mind, and will not be effective.

Put your whole mind into present action.

Do not give your creative impulse to Divine Substance, and then sit down and wait for results; if you do, you will never get them. *Act now.* There is never any time but now, and there never will be any time but now. If you are ever to begin to make ready for the reception of what you want, you must begin now.

And your action, whatever it is, must most likely be in your present business or employment, and must be upon the persons and things in your present environment.

You cannot act where you are not; you cannot act where you have been, and you cannot act where you are going to be; you can act only where you are.

Do not bother as to whether yesterday's work was well done or ill done; do today's work well.

Do not try to do tomorrow's work now; there will be plenty of time to do that when you get to it.

Do not try, by occult or mystical means, to act on people or things that are out of your reach.

Do not wait for a change of environment, before you act. Get a change of environment by action.

You can so act upon the environment in which you are now, as to cause yourself to be transferred to a better environment.

Hold with faith and purpose the vision of yourself in the better environment, but act upon your present environment with all your heart, and with all your strength, and with all your mind.

Do not spend any time in daydreaming or castle building; hold to the one vision of what you want, and act *now*.

Do not cast about seeking some new thing to do, or some strange, unusual, or remarkable action to perform as a first step toward getting rich. It is probable that your actions, at least for some time to come will be those you have been performing for some time past; but you are to begin now to perform these actions in the Certain Way, which will surely make you rich.

If you are engaged in some business, and feel that it is not the right one for you, do not wait until you get into the right business before you begin to act.

Do not feel discouraged, or sit down and lament because you are misplaced. No one was ever so misplaced but that he or she could not find the right place, and no one ever became so involved in the wrong business that it was not possible to get into the right business.

Hold the vision of yourself in the right business, with the purpose to get into it and the faith that you will get into it, and are getting into it. *Act* in your present business. Use your present business as the means of getting a better one, and use your present environment as the means of getting into a better one. Your vision of the right business, if held with faith and purpose, will cause the Supreme to move the right business toward you; and your action, if performed in the Certain Way, will cause you to move toward the business.

If you are an employee, or wage earner, and feel that you must change places in order to get what you want, do not project your thought into space and rely upon it to get you another job. It will probably fail to do so.

Hold the vision of yourself in the job you want, while you *act* with faith and purpose on the job you have, and you will certainly get the job you want.

Your vision and faith will set the creative force in motion to bring it toward you, and your action will cause the forces in your own environment to move you toward the place you want. In closing this chapter, another statement is added to the syllabus—

- *There is a thinking stuff from which all things are made, and which, in its original state, permeates, penetrates, and fills the interspaces of the universe.*
- *A thought, in this substance, produces the thing that is imaged by the thought.*
- *We can form things in our thought, and, by impressing our thought upon Divine substance, can cause the thing we think about to be created.*
- *In order to do this, we must pass from the competitive to the creative mind; We must form a clear mental picture of the things we want, and hold this picture in our thoughts with the fixed* purpose *to get what we want and the unwavering* faith *that we do get what we want, closing our mind to all that may tend to shake our purpose, dim our vision, or quench our faith.*
- *That we may receive what we want when it comes, we must act* now *upon the people and things in our present environment.*

Chapter

12

EFFICIENT ACTION

You must use your thought as directed in previous chapters, and begin to do what you can do where you are; and you must do *all* that you can do where you are.

You can advance only by being larger than your present place; and you cannot be larger than your present place if you leave undone any of the work pertaining to that place.

The world is advanced only by those who more than fill their present places.

If we cannot fill our present place, everything will go backwards. Those who do not quite fill their present places are dead weight upon society, government, commerce, and industry; others must carry them along at a great expense. The progress of the world is retarded only by those who do not fill the places they are holding. They belong to a former age and a lower stage or plane of life, and their tendency is toward degeneration. No society could advance if each of us was smaller than our place. The law of physical and mental evolution guides social evolution. In the animal world, evolution is caused by excess of life.

When an organism has more life than can be expressed in the functions of its own plane, it develops the organs of a higher plane, and a new species is originated.

There never would have been new species had there not been organisms that more than filled their places. The law is exactly the same for you; your getting rich depends upon your applying this principle to your own affairs.

Every day is either a successful day or a day of failure; and it is the successful days that get you what you want. If every day is a failure, you can never get rich; while if every day is a success, you cannot fail to get rich.

If there is something that may be done today, and you do not do it, you have failed in so far as that thing is concerned; and the consequences may be more disastrous than you imagine.

You cannot foresee the results of even the most trivial act; you do not know the workings of all the forces that have been set moving in your behalf. Much may be depending on your doing some simple act; it may be the very thing that is to open the door of opportunity to very great possibilities. You can never know all the combinations that Supreme Intelligence is making for you in the world of things and of human affairs. Your neglect or failure to do some small thing may cause a long delay in getting what you want.

Do, every day all that can be done that day.

There is, however, a limitation or qualification of the above that you must take into account.

You are not to overwork or to rush blindly into your business in the effort to do the greatest possible number of things in the shortest possible time.

You are not to try to do tomorrow's work today, nor to do a week's work in a day.

It is really not the number of things you do, but the efficiency *of each separate action that counts.*

Every act is, in itself, either a success or a failure. Every act is, in itself, either effective or inefficient.

Every inefficient act is a failure, and if you spend your life in doing inefficient acts, your whole life will be a failure.

The more things you do, the worse for you if all your acts are inefficient ones.

On the other hand, every efficient act is a success in itself, and if every act of your life is an efficient one, your whole life *must* be a success.

The cause of failure is doing too many things in an inefficient manner, and not doing enough things in an efficient manner.

You will see that it is a self-evident proposition that if you do not do any inefficient acts, and if you do a sufficient number of efficient acts, you will become rich. If, now, it is possible for you to make each act an efficient one, you see again that the getting of riches is reduced to an exact science, like mathematics.

The matter turns, then, on the questions whether you can make each separate act a success in itself. And this you can certainly do.

You can make each act a success, because God's power is working with you; and God's power cannot fail.

God's power is at your service; and to make each act efficient you have only to put that power into it.

Every action is either strong or weak; and when everyone is strong, you are acting in the Certain Way, which will make you rich.

Every act can be made strong and efficient by holding your vision while you are doing it, and putting the whole power of your *faith* and *purpose* into it.

It is at this point that the people fail who separate mental power from personal action. They use the power of mind in one place and at one time, and they act in another pace and at another time. So their acts are not successful in themselves. Too many of them are inefficient. But if God's Power goes into every act, no matter how commonplace, every act will be a success in itself. As in the nature of things every success opens the way to other successes, your progress toward what you want, and the progress of what you want toward you, will become increasingly rapid.

Remember that successful action is cumulative in its results. Since the desire for more life is inherent in all things, when you begin to move toward larger life more things attach themselves to you, and the influence of your desire is multiplied.

Do, every day, all that you can do that day, and do each act in an efficient manner.

You must hold your vision while you are doing each act, however trivial or commonplace. This does not mean that it is necessary at all times to see the vision distinctly to its smallest details. It should be the work of your leisure hours to use your imagination on the details of your vision, and to contemplate them until they are firmly fixed upon memory. If you wish speedy results, spend practically all your spare time in this practice.

By continuous contemplation you will get the picture of what you want, even to the smallest details. It will be so firmly fixed upon your mind, and so completely transferred to the mind of Divine Substance, that in your working hours you need only to mentally refer to the picture to stimulate your faith and purpose, and cause your best effort to be put forth. Contemplate your picture in your leisure hours until your consciousness is so full of it that you can grasp it instantly. You will become so enthused with its bright promises that the mere thought of it will call forth the strongest energies of your whole being.

Let us again repeat our syllabus, and by slightly changing the closing statements bring it to the point we have now reached.

- *There is a thinking stuff from which all things are made, and which, in its original state, permeates, penetrates, and fills the interspaces of the universe.*
- *A thought, in this substance, produces the thing that is imaged by the thought.*
- *We can form things in our thought, and, by impressing our thought upon Divine substance, can cause the thing we think about to be created.*
- *In order to do this, we must pass from the competitive to the creative mind; we must form a clear mental picture of the things we want, and do, with faith and purpose, all that can be done each day, doing each separate thing in an efficient manner.*

Chapter
13

GETTING INTO
THE RIGHT BUSINESS

Success, in any particular business, depends for one thing upon your possessing in a well-developed state the faculties required in that business.

Without good musical faculty no one can succeed as a teacher of music; without well-developed mechanical faculties no one can achieve great success in any of the mechanical trades; without tact and the commercial faculties no one can succeed in mercantile pursuits. But to possess in a well-developed state the faculties required in your particular vocation does not insure getting rich. There are musicians who have remarkable talent, and who yet remain poor; there are blacksmiths, carpenters, and so on who have excellent mechanical ability, but who do not get rich; and there are merchants with good faculties for dealing with men who nevertheless fail.

The different faculties are tools. It is essential to have good tools, but it is also essential that the tools should be used in the Right Way. One carpenter can take a sharp saw, a square, a good plane, and so on, and build a handsome article of furniture; another carpenter can take the same tools and set to work to duplicate the article, but the production will be a botch. That carpenter does not know how to use good tools in a successful way.

The various faculties of your mind are the tools with which you must do the work that is to make you rich. It will be easier for you to succeed if you get into a business for which you are well equipped with mental tools.

Generally speaking, you will do best in that business which will use your strongest faculties – the one for which you are naturally 'best fitted.' But there are limitations to this statement, also. We never should regard our vocation as being irrevocably fixed by the tendencies with which we were born.

You can get rich in *any* business. Even if you do not have the right talent, you can develop that talent. It merely means that you will have to make your tools as you go along, instead of confining yourself to the use of those with which you were born. It will be *easier* for you to succeed in a vocation for which you already have the talents in a well-developed state; but you *can* succeed in any vocation. You can develop any rudimentary talent, and there is no talent of which you have not at least the rudiment.

You will get rich most easily in point of effort, if you do that for which you are best fitted; but you will get rich most satisfactorily if you do that which you *want* to do.

Doing what you want to do is life; and there is no real satisfaction in living if we are compelled to be forever doing something that we do not like to do, and can never do what we want to do. And it is certain that you can do what you want to do. The *desire* to do it is proof that you have within you the power that *can* do it.

Desire is a manifestation of power.

The desire to play music is the power that can play music seeking expression and development; the desire to invent mechanical devices is the mechanical talent seeking expression and development.

Where there is no power, either developed or undeveloped, to do a thing, there is never any desire to do that thing. Where there is strong desire to do a thing, it is certain proof that the power to do it is strong, and only requires developing and applying it in the Right Way.

All things else being equal, it is best to select the business for which you have the best developed talent. However, if you have a strong desire to engage in any particular line of work, you should select that work as the ultimate end at which you aim.

You can do what you want to do, and it is your right and privilege to follow the business or avocation that will be most congenial and pleasant.

You are not obliged to do what you do not like to do, and should not do it except as a means to bring you to the doing of the thing you want to do.

If there are past mistakes whose consequences have placed you in an undesirable business or environment, you may be obliged for some time to do what you do not like to do. However, you can make the doing of it pleasant by knowing that it is making it possible for you to come to the doing of what you want to do.

If you feel that you are not in the right vocation, do not act too hastily in trying to get into another one. The best way, generally, to change business or environment is by growth.

Do not be afraid to make a sudden and radical change if the opportunity is presented, and you feel after careful consideration that it is the right opportunity; but never take sudden or radical action when you are in doubt as to the wisdom of doing so.

There is never any hurry on the creative plane; and there is no lack of opportunity.

When you get out of the competitive mind you will understand that you never need to act hastily. No one else is going to beat you to the thing you want to do; there is enough for all. If one space is taken, another and a better one will be opened for you a little farther on; there is plenty of time. When you are in doubt, wait. Fall back on the contemplation of your vision, and increase your faith and purpose; and by all means, in times of doubt and indecision, cultivate gratitude.

A day or two spent in contemplating the vision of what you want, and in earnest thanksgiving that you are getting it, will bring your mind into such close relationship with the Supreme that you will make no mistake when you do act.

There is a mind that knows all there is to know; and you can come into close unity with this mind by faith and the purpose to advance in life, if you have deep gratitude.

Mistakes come from acting hastily, or from acting in fear or doubt, or in forgetfulness of the Right Motive, which is more life to all, and less to none.

As you go on in the Certain Way, opportunities will come to you in increasing number; and you will need to be very steady in your faith and purpose, and to keep in close touch with God by reverent gratitude.

Do all that you can do in a perfect manner every day, but do it without haste, worry, or fear. Go as fast as you can, but never hurry.

Remember that in the moment you begin to hurry you cease to be a creator and become a competitor; you drop back upon the old plane again.

Whenever you find yourself hurrying, call a halt; fix your attention on the mental image of the thing you want, and begin to give thanks that you are getting it. The exercise of *gratitude* will never fail to strengthen your faith and renew your purpose.

Chapter

14

THE IMPRESSION OF INCREASE

Whether you change your vocation or not, your actions for the present must be those pertaining to the business in which you are now engaged.

You can get into the business you want by making constructive use of the business you are already established in by doing your daily work in a Certain Way.

And in so far as your business consists in dealing with others, whether personally or by letter, the key-thought of all your efforts must be to convey to their minds the impression of increase.

Increase is what all men and all women are seeking; it is the urge of the Divine Intelligence within them, seeking fuller expression.

The desire for increase is inherent in all nature; it is the fundamental impulse of the universe. All human activities are based on the desire for increase; people are seeking more food, more clothes, better shelter, more luxury, more beauty, more knowledge, more pleasure – increase in something, more life.

Every living thing is under this necessity for continuous advancement; where increase of life ceases, dissolution and death set in at once.

However love of money to the exclusion of everything else will cause you to become lopsided and unbalanced. You are here to use your power or authority wisely. Some people crave power; others crave money. If you set your heart on money, and say 'That's all I want. I am going to give all my attention to amassing money; nothing else matters,' you can get money and attain a fortune, but you have forgotten that you are here to lead a balanced life. 'Man does not live by bread alone.'

If all your time is devoted to external things and possessions, you will find yourself hungry for peace of mind, harmony, love, joy or perfect health. You will find that you cannot buy anything that is real. You can amass a fortune, or have millions of dollars. This is not evil or bad. Love of money to the exclusion of everything else results in frustration, disappointment and disillusionment. In that sense it is the root of your evil.

The normal desire for increased wealth is not an evil or a reprehensible thing; it is simply the desire for more abundant life; it is aspiration.

And because it is the deepest instinct of their natures, all men and women are attracted to those who can give them more of the means of life.

In following the Certain Way as described in the foregoing pages, you are getting continuous increase for yourself, and you are giving it to all with whom you deal.

You are a creative center, from which increase is given off to all.

Be sure of this, and convey assurance of the fact to every man, woman, and child with whom you come in contact. No matter how small the transaction, even if it were only the selling of a stick of candy to a little child, put into it the thought of increase, and make sure that the customer is impressed with the thought.

Convey the impression of advancement with everything you do, so that all people shall receive the impression that you are an Advancing Thinker and that you advance all who deal with you. Even to the people whom you meet in a social way, without any thought of business, and to whom you do not try to sell anything, give the thought of increase.

You can convey this impression by holding the unshakable faith that you, yourself, are in the Way of Increase; and by letting this faith inspire, fill, and permeate every action.

Do everything that you do in the firm conviction that you are an advancing personality, and that you are giving advancement to everybody.

Feel that you are getting rich, and that in so doing you are making others rich, and conferring benefits on all.

Do not boast or brag of your success, or talk about it unnecessarily; true faith is never boastful.

Wherever you find a boastful person, you find one who is secretly doubtful and afraid. Simply feel the faith, and let it work out in every transaction; let every act and tone and look express the quiet assurance that you are getting rich; that you are already rich. Words will not be necessary to communicate this feeling to others; they will feel the sense of increase when in your presence, and will be attracted to you again.

You must so impress others that they will feel that in associating with you they will get increase for themselves. See that you give them a use value greater than the cash value you are taking from them.

Take an honest pride in doing this, and let everybody know it; and you will have no lack of customers. People will go where they are given increase; and the Supreme God, which desires increase in all, and which knows all, will move toward you men and women who have never heard of you. Your business will increase rapidly, and you will be surprised at the unexpected benefits that will come to you. You will be able from day to day to make larger combinations, secure greater advantages, and to go on into a more congenial vocation if you desire to do so.

But doing thing all this, you must never lose sight of your vision of what you want, or your faith and purpose to get what you want.

Now, another word of caution in regard to motives. Beware of the insidious temptation to seek for power over others.

Nothing is as pleasant to the unformed or partially developed mind as the exercise of power or dominion over others. *The desire to rule for selfish gratification has been the curse of the world*. For countless ages kings and lords have drenched the earth with blood in their battles to extend their dominions. This was not to seek more life for all, but to get more power for themselves.

Today, the main motive in the business and industrial world is the same. Armies of dollars are marshaled. The lives and hearts of millions are wasted in the mad scramble for power over others. Commercial kings, like political kings, are inspired by the lust for power.

Look out for the temptation to seek for authority, to become a 'master,' to be considered as one who is above the common herd, to impress others by lavish display, and so on.

The mind that seeks for mastery over others is the competitive mind; and the competitive mind is not the creative one. In order to master your environment and your destiny, it is not at all necessary that you should rule over others. Indeed, when you fall into the world's struggle for the high places, you begin to be conquered by fate and environment, and your getting rich becomes a matter of chance and speculation.

Beware of the competitive mind! No better statement of the principle of creative action can be formulated than this variation of the Golden Rule: 'What I want for myself, I want for everybody.'

Chapter
15

THE ADVANCING THINKER

What was said in the last chapter applies as well to people in the professions, wage earners, and those engaged in mercantile businesses.

No matter whether you are a physician, a teacher, or a clergyman, if you can give increase of life to others and make them sensible of the fact, they will be attracted to you, and you will get rich. Physicians who hold the vision of themselves as great and successful healers, and who work toward the complete realization of that vision with faith and purpose, as described in former chapters, will come into such close touch with the Source of Life that they will be phenomenally successful; patients will come to them in throngs.

In the field of religion, the world cries out for clergy who can teach their hearers the true science of abundant life. Those who master the details of the science of getting rich, together with the allied sciences of being well, of being great, and of winning love, and who teach these details from the pulpit, will never lack for a congregation. This is the gospel that the world needs; it will give increase of life, and congregants will hear it gladly, and will give liberal support to those who bring it to them.

What is now needed is a demonstration of the science of life from the pulpit. We want preachers, rabbis, priests and imams who can not only tell us how, but who in their own persons will show us how. We need clergy who will themselves be rich, healthy, great, and beloved, to teach us how to attain to these things. Such leaders will find a numerous and loyal following.

The same is true of teachers who can inspire the children with the faith and purpose of the advancing life. They will never be out of a job. All teachers who have this faith and purpose can give it to their pupils. They cannot help giving it to them if it is part of their own lives and practice.

What is true of the teacher, preacher, and physician is true of the lawyer, dentist, realtor, insurance agent – of everybody.

This combined mental and personal action is infallible; it cannot fail. Every man and woman, who follows these instructions steadily, perseveringly, and to the letter, will get rich. The law of the Increase of Life is as mathematically certain in its operation as the law of gravitation. Getting rich is an exact science.

Wage earners will find this as true of their case as of any of the others mentioned. Do not feel that you have no chance to get rich because you are working where there is no visible opportunity for advancement, where wages are small and the cost of living high. Form your clear mental vision of what you want, and begin to act with faith and purpose.

Do all the work you can do, every day, and do each piece of work in a perfectly successful manner. Put the power of success, and the purpose to get rich, into everything that you do.

But do not do this merely with the idea of currying favor with those above you, in the hope that they will see your good work and advance you; it is not likely that they will do so.

Employees who are merely 'good' workers, performing the very best of their ability, and satisfied with that, are valuable to their employers, but it is not to the employers' interest to promote such people as they are worth more where being kept where they are.

To secure advancement, something more is necessary than to be too large for your place.

Those workers who are certain to advance are those who are too big for their current job, and who have a clear concept of what they want to be. They know that they can become what they want to be and are determined to *be* what they want to be.

Do not try to more than fill your present place with a view to pleasing your employer; do it with the idea of advancing yourself. Hold the faith and purpose of increase during work hours, after work hours, and before work hours. Hold it in such a way that every person who comes in contact with you, whether supervisor, another worker, or social acquaintance, will feel the power of purpose radiating from you; so that everyone will get the sense of advancement and increase from you. Other people will be attracted to you, and if there is no possibility for advancement in your present job, you will very soon see an opportunity to take another job.

There is a Power that never fails to present opportunity to the Advancing Thinker who is moving in obedience to law.

God cannot help helping you, if you act in a Certain Way; He must do so in order to help Himself.

There is nothing in your circumstances or in the industrial situation that can keep you down. If you cannot get rich working in an automobile factory, you can get rich owning and managing a fast food franchise. If you begin to move in the Certain Way, you will certainly escape from the 'clutches' of the auto factory and open that restaurant or wherever else you wish to do.

If a few thousands of its employees would enter upon the Certain Way, the large manufacturers would soon be in a bad plight. It would have to give its workers more opportunity, or go out of business. Nobody has to work for a giant corporation. Such firms can keep workers in so called hopeless conditions only so long as there are people who are too ignorant to know of the science of getting rich, or too intellectually slothful to practice it.

Begin this way of thinking and acting and your faith and purpose will make you quick to see any opportunity to better your condition.

Such opportunities will speedily come, for the Supreme God, with all His power is working with you, will bring them before you.

Do not wait for an opportunity to be all that you want to be. When an opportunity to be more than you are now is presented and you feel impelled toward it, take it. It will be the first step toward a greater opportunity.

There is no such thing possible in this universe as a lack of opportunities for those who are living the advancing life.

It is inherent in the constitution of the cosmos that all things shall be for us and will work together for our good. We must certainly get rich if we act and think in the Certain Way. So let wage earners study this book with great care, and enter with confidence upon the course of action it prescribes; it will not fail.

Chapter
16

SOME CAUTIONS AND CONCLUDING OBSERVATIONS

Many people will scoff at the idea that there is an exact science of getting rich; holding the impression that the supply of wealth is limited, they will insist that social and governmental institutions must be changed before even any considerable number of people can acquire a competence.

But this is not true.

It is true that existing governments may keep the masses in poverty, but this is because the masses do not think and act in the Certain Way.

If the masses begin to move forward as suggested in this book, neither governments nor industrial systems can check them; all systems must be modified to accommodate the forward movement.

If the people have the New Thought, the Advancing Mind, and have the Faith that they can become rich, and move forward with the fixed purpose to become rich, nothing can possibly keep them in poverty.

Individuals may enter upon the Certain Way at any time, and under any government, and make themselves rich. When any considerable numbers of individuals do so under any government, they will cause the system to be so modified as to open the way for others.

The more people who get rich on the competitive plane, the worse for others; the more who get rich on the creative plane, the better for others.

The economic salvation of the masses can only be accomplished by getting a large number of people to practice the scientific method set down in this book and become rich. These will show others the way, and inspire them with a desire for real life, with the faith that it can be attained, and with the purpose to attain it.

For the present, however, it is enough to know that neither the government under which you live nor the capitalistic or competitive system of industry can keep you from getting rich. When you enter upon the creative plane of thought you will rise above all these things and become a citizen of another kingdom.

But remember that your thought must be held upon the creative plane; you are never for an instant to be betrayed into regarding the supply as limited, or into acting on the moral level of competition.

Whenever you do fall into old ways of thought, correct yourself instantly; for when you are in the competitive mind, you have lost the cooperation of the Mind of the Whole.

Do not spend any time in planning as to how you will meet possible emergencies in the future, except as the necessary policies may affect your actions today. You are concerned with doing today's work in a perfectly successful manner, and not with emergencies that may arise tomorrow; you can attend to them as they come.

Do not concern yourself with questions as to how you shall surmount obstacles that may loom upon your business horizon, unless you can see plainly that your course must be altered today in order to avoid them.

No matter how tremendous an obstruction may appear at a distance, you will find that if you go on in the Certain Way it will disappear as you approach it, or that a way over, though, or around it will appear.

No possible combination of circumstances can defeat a man or woman who is proceeding to get rich along strictly scientific lines. No man or woman who obeys the law can fail to get rich, any more than one can multiply two by two and fail to get four.

Give no anxious thought to possible disasters, obstacles, panics, or unfavorable combinations of circumstances; it is time enough to meet such things when they present themselves before you in the immediate present, and you will find that every difficulty carries with it the wherewithal for its overcoming.

Guard your speech. Never speak of yourself, your affairs, or of anything else in a discouraged or discouraging way.

Never admit the possibility of failure, or speak in a way that infers failure as a possibility.

Never speak of the times as being hard, or of business conditions as being doubtful. Times may be hard and business doubtful for those who are on the competitive plane, but they can never be so for you; you can create what you want, and you are above fear.

When others are having hard times and poor business, you will find your greatest opportunities.

Train yourself to think of and to look upon the world as a something that is constantly developing and growing; and to regard seeming evil as being only, that which is undeveloped. Always speak in terms of advancement; to do otherwise is to deny your faith, and to deny your faith is to lose it.

Never allow yourself to feel disappointed. You may expect to have a certain thing at a certain time, and not get it at that time; and this will appear to you like failure.

But if you hold to your faith you will find that the failure is only apparent.

Go on in the certain way, and if you do not receive that thing, you will receive something so much better that you will see that the seeming failure was really a great success.

A student of this science had set his mind on making a certain business combination that seemed to him at the time to be very desirable, and he worked for some, weeks to bring it about. When the crucial time came, the thing failed in a perfectly inexplicable way. It was as if some unseen influence had been working secretly against him. He was not disappointed; on the contrary, he thanked God that his desire had been overruled, and went steadily on with a grateful mind. In a few weeks an opportunity so much better came his way that he would not have made the first deal on any account; and he saw that a Mind which knew more than he knew had prevented him from losing the greater good by entangling himself with the lesser.

That is the way every seeming failure will work out for you, if you keep your faith, hold to your purpose, and have gratitude, and do, every day all that can be done that day, doing each separate act in a successful manner.

When you make a failure, it is because you have not asked for enough. Keep on, and a larger thing then you were seeking will certainly come to you.

Remember this.

You will not fail because you lack the necessary talent to do what you wish to do. If you go on as this book has directed, you will develop all the talent that is necessary to the doing of your work.

It is not within the scope of this book to deal with the science of cultivating talent; but it is as certain and simple as the process of getting rich.

However, do not hesitate or waver for fear that when you come to any certain place you will fail for lack of ability; keep right on, and when you come to that place, the ability will be furnished to you. The same source of ability that enabled the untaught Lincoln to do the greatest work in government ever accomplished by a single man is open to you. You may draw upon universal wisdom in meeting the responsibilities that are laid upon you. Go on in full faith.

Study this book. Make it your constant companion until you have mastered all the ideas contained in it. While you are getting firmly established in this faith, you will do well to give up most recreations and pleasure and to stay away from places where ideas conflicting with these are advanced in lectures or sermons. Do not read pessimistic or conflicting literature, or get into arguments upon the matter. Spend most of your leisure time in contemplating your vision, and in cultivating gratitude, and in reading this book. It contains all you need to know of the science of getting rich; and you will find all the essentials summed up in the following chapter.

Chapter
17

SUMMARY OF THE SCIENCE OF GETTING RICH

There is a thinking stuff from which all things are made, and which, in its original state, permeates, penetrates, and fills the interspaces of the universe.

A thought in this substance produces the thing that is imaged by the thought.

We can form things in our thought, and by impressing our thought upon Divine substance can cause the thing we think about to be created.

In order to do this, we must pass from the competitive to the creative mind; otherwise we cannot be in harmony with the Divine Intelligence, which is always creative and never competitive in spirit.

We may come into full harmony with the Divine Substance by entertaining a lively and sincere gratitude for the blessings it bestows upon us. Gratitude unifies our minds with the intelligence of Substance, so our thoughts are received by the Divine. We can remain upon the creative plane only by uniting ourselves with the Divine Intelligence through a deep and continuous feeling of gratitude.

We must form a clear and definite mental image of the things we wish to have, to do, or to become. We must hold this mental image in our thoughts, while being deeply grateful to the Supreme that all our desires are granted to us. If we wish to get rich, we must spend our leisure hours in contemplating our Vision, and in earnest thanksgiving that the reality is being given to us. Too much stress cannot be laid on the importance of frequent contemplation of the mental image, coupled with unwavering faith and devout gratitude. This is the process by which the impression is given to the Divine, and the creative forces set in motion.

The creative energy works through the established channels of natural growth, and of the industrial and social order. All that is included in this mental image will surely be brought to those who follow the instructions given above, and whose faith does not waver. What we want will come to us through the ways of established trade and commerce.

In order to receive our own when it shall come to us, we must be active; and this activity can only consist in more than just filling our present place. We must keep in mind our purpose is to get rich through the realization of our mental image. Therefore, we must do, every day, all that can be done that day, taking care to do each act in a successful manner. We must give to every person a use value in excess of the cash value he or she receives, so that each transaction makes for more life. Most of all we must so hold the New Thought that the impression of increase will be communicated to all with whom we come in contact. This is the secret of attaining wealth. Practice the foregoing instructions and you will certainly get rich.

PART II

THE SCIENCE OF BEING GREAT

PREFACE

What does it mean to be great? Some people look upon others as great because they are famous. Movie and TV stars, sports celebrities, elected officials, business tycoons are recognized, admired and often idolized. But are they truly great?

Greatness is more than fame; it's more than wealth; it's more than just being an achiever. A great person is one who has earned the respect and admiration of others by the way he or she thinks, acts and lives his or her life. You need not be famous to be great. Indeed, many great people are known only to their family, friends and neighbors.

You should not attempt great things until you are ready to do them in a great way. If you undertake to deal with great matters in a small way—that is, from a low viewpoint or with incomplete consecration and wavering faith and courage—you will fail. Do not be in a hurry to get to the great things. Doing great things will not make you great, but becoming great will certainly lead you to the doing of great things. Begin to be great where you are and in the things you do every day. Do not be in haste to be found out or recognized as a great personality. Do not be disappointed if you are not nominated for office within a month after you begin to practice what you read in this book. Great people never seek recognition or applause; they are not great because they want to be paid for being so. Greatness is reward enough for itself. The joy of being something and of knowing that you are advancing is the greatest of all joys possible.

You do not have to go charging about the world like Don Quixote, tilting at windmills, and overturning things in general, in order to demonstrate that you are somebody. It is not necessary to go hunting for big things to do. All you must do – and you must truly do this – is too live a great life where you are, and in your daily activities, and greater works will surely find you out. Big things will come to you, asking to be done.

Follow the steps described in the following chapters and it will not be long before your family and friends will begin to defer, more and more, to your judgment and to be guided by you. Soon your neighbors and townspeople will be coming to you for counsel and advice; soon you will be recognized as one who is great in small things, and you will be called upon more and more to take charge of larger things.

Truly great people will let this deference and respect affect their ego. You must cast out pride and vanity, and have no thought of trying to rule over others or of outdoing them. This is a vital point; there is no temptation so insidious as the selfish desire to rule over others. Nothing so appeals to the average man or woman as to sit in the uppermost places at feasts, to be respectfully saluted in the. marketplace, and to be called 'My Lord', 'Your Excellency' or 'Master'. To exercise some sort of control over others is the secret motive of every selfish person. The struggle for power over others is the battle of the competitive world, and you must rise above that world and its motives and aspirations and seek only for life. Cast out envy; you can have all that you want, and you need not envy any person what he or she has. Above all things, see to it that you do not hold malice or enmity toward anyone; to do so cuts you off from the mind whose treasures you to seek to make your own. Lay aside all narrow personal ambition – and determine to seek the highest good aid to be swayed by no unworthy selfishness.

You must learn not to look upon the world as a lost and decaying thing but as a something perfect and glorious, which is going on to a most beautiful completeness. You must learn to see men and women not as lost and accursed things, but as perfect beings advancing to become complete.

Let your attitude in business, in politics, in neighborhood affairs, and in your own home be the expression of the best thoughts you can think. Let your manner toward all men and women, great and small, and especially to your own family circle, always be the most kindly, gracious, and courteous you can picture in your imagination. Remember your viewpoint; you are a god in the company of gods and must conduct yourself accordingly.

Study carefully the secrets of achieving greatness that you will find in the following pages. Practice what you read. Greatness will not be thrust upon you, but step by step, you will inexorably move to the point where you will be respected, admired and looked upon as a great person.

Chapter

1

ANY PERSON MAY BECOME GREAT

There is a Principle of Power in each of us. By the intelligent use and direction of this principle, we can develop our own mental faculties. We have an inherent power by which we may grow in whatsoever direction we please, and there does not appear to be any limit to the possibilities of our growth. None of us have as yet become so great in any faculty but that it is possible for someone else to become greater. The possibility is in the Divine Substance from which we are made.

Great people are always greater than their deeds. They connected with reserve power that is without limit. We do not know the boundary of our mental power; we do not even know that there is a boundary.

The power of conscious growth is not given to the lower animals. It is reserved for humankind alone. The lower animals can, to a great extent, be trained and developed by us, we only we have the power to train and develop ourselves, and have it to an apparently unlimited extent.

The purpose of our life is growth, just as the purpose of life for trees and plants is growth. Trees and plants grow automatically and along fixed lines. We humans can grow, as we will. Trees and plants can only develop certain possibilities and characteristics; we can develop any power that is or has been shown by any person, anywhere. Nothing that is possible in spirit is impossible in flesh and blood. Nothing that we can think is impossible in action. Nothing that we can imagine is impossible of realization.

We are formed for growth, and we are under the necessity of growing. It is essential to our happiness that we should continuously advance. Life without progress becomes unendurable, and the person who ceases from growth must either become imbecile or insane. The greater and more harmonious and well-rounded our growth, the happier we will be.

There is no possibility in any person that is not in all people; but if they proceed naturally, no two people will grow into the same thing, or be alike.

Each of us comes into the world with a predisposition to grow along certain lines, and growth is easier for us along those lines than any other way. This is a wise provision because it gives endless variety. It is as if a gardener should throw all his bulbs into one basket; to the superficial observer they would look alike, but growth reveals a tremendous difference. So of men and women; they are like the basket of bulbs. One may be a rose and add brightness and color to some dark corner of the world; one may be a climbing vine and hide the rugged outlines of some dark rock; one may be a great oak among whose boughs the birds shall nest and sing, and beneath whose shade the flocks shall rest at noon, but everyone will be something worthwhile, something rare, something perfect.

There are undreamed of possibilities in the common lives all around us. In a large sense, there are no 'common' people. In times of national stress and peril even the simplest individuals may become heroes and statesmen through the quickening of the Principle of Power within them. There is a genius in every man and woman, waiting to be brought forth. Every village has some great men or women; people to whom all go for advice in time of trouble; people who are instinctively recognized as being great in wisdom and insight. To such people the minds of the whole community turn in times of local crisis. Those people are tacitly recognized as being great. They do small things in a great way. They could do great things as well if they did but undertake them; so can any person; so can you. The Principle of Power gives us just what we ask of it; if we only undertake little things, it only gives us power for little things; but if we try to do great thing in a great way it gives us the power there is. But beware of undertaking great things in a small way; of that we shall speak farther on.

There are two mental attitudes we may take. One makes us like a football. It has resilience and reacts strongly when force is applied to it, but it originates nothing; it never acts of itself. There is no power within it. People of this type are controlled by circumstances and environment. Their destinies are decided by things external to themselves. The Principle of Power within them is never really active at all. They never speak or act from within. The other attitude makes people like a flowing spring. Power comes out from the center of them. They have within themselves a well of water springing up into everlasting life. They radiate force. They are felt by their environment. The Principle of Power in them is in constant action. They are self-active.

No greater good can come to any man or woman than to become self-active. All the experiences of life are designed by Providence to force men and women into self-activity; to compel them to cease being creatures of circumstances and master their environment. In the lowest stage of our lives, we are children of chance and circumstance and the slave of fear. Our acts are all reactions resulting from the impingement upon us of forces in our environment. We act only as we are acted upon. We originate nothing. But within themselves a Principle of Power sufficient to master all that they fear and if they learn this and become self-active, they become as one of the gods.

Nothing was ever in any human being that is not in you; no one ever had more spiritual or mental power than you can attain, or did greater things than you can accomplish. The New Thought concept can be summed up in these words: *You can become what you want to be.*

Arnold Schwarzenegger is a good example of a person who knew what he wanted to be and converted his desire into action and achievement. He first came into the public eye as 'Mr. Universe,' a glorified weight lifter.

But Schwarzenegger was not a typical 'muscle man.' He was a man with dreams and goals – and he achieved them to become a very wealthy businessman and one of the highest paid movie stars and eventually governor of California.

He was born and raised in Austria and as a child began training as a weight lifter. At 18, he won his first bodybuilding contest and won the first of five straight Mr. Universe titles. He emigrated to the United States and continued winning similar contests.

Although he had accomplished more than any other person had in the art of bodybuilding, it was no longer a challenge. He sought other areas where he could use his talents.

His training in physical development taught him that there was a need for knowledge about physical fitness and he had that knowledge and wanted to share it.

He wrote an autobiography – *Arnold: The Education of a Bodybuilder,* which became a bestseller. He followed it with a book on body building for women – showing female readers how to use weight training to get in shape.

This led to the creation of a mail-order exercise business, and a company to produce bodybuilding events. These businesses started him on the road to business success.

His next goal was to become a movie star. Even before he had his first movie role, he set as a goal to be as big in movies as he was in bodybuilding.

After turning down minor roles, his persistence paid off when he was cast as the lead in *Conan the Barbarian.* This led to a series of additional action films that made him one of the highest paid actors in Hollywood.

Success in the movies did not make Schwarzenegger complacent. He set new goals for himself, this time in the world of business. He invested in real estate, created a restaurant chain and became actively involved in other enterprises, and became a multi-millionaire.

However, as his successes mounted, he added what became his dream goal – to serve the community. He traveled around the country to promote health and fitness for youth. He went into the inner cities and inspired the kids to eschew violence and crime, and to say no to drugs and guns and gangs and say yes to education.

Schwarzenegger has met this goal by funding and taking an active leadership role in several organizations dedicated to physical fitness and health. He has served on the President's commission for physical fitness that sets standards of fitness for the entire country.

In 2003, when the people of California voted to recall the incumbent governor, Schwarzenegger threw his hat into the ring and was overwhelmingly elected as the new governor.

You can learn much from this man. In setting goals, you are not limited to anyone area. Schwarzenegger could have limited his future to bodybuilding and become quite successful, but he dreamed of much more, set higher goals and strove to reach them. He learned from his successes and adapted this knowledge in other aspects of his life.

Do not be discouraged by criticism. Critics belittled his acting ability in his first films, but he was not dissuaded and pursued his goals to become a major movie star, and later a very successful entrepreneur and governor of America's most populous state.

Chapter

2

HEREDITY AND OPPORTUNITY

You are not barred from attaining greatness by heredity. No matter who or what your ancestors may have been or how unlearned or lowly their station, the upward way is open for you. There is no such thing as inheriting a fixed mental position. No matter how small the mental capital we receive from our parents, it may be increased. No one is born incapable of growth.

Heredity counts for something. We are born with subconscious mental tendencies — for instance, a tendency to melancholy, or cowardice, or to ill-temper, but all these subconscious tendencies may be overcome. You can throw them off very easily. Nothing of this kind need keep you down. If you have inherited undesirable mental tendencies, you can eliminate them and put desirable tendencies in their places. An inherited mental trait is a habit of thought of your father or mother impressed upon your subconscious mind. You can substitute the opposite impression by forming the opposite habit of thought. You can substitute a habit of cheerfulness for a tendency to despondency. You can overcome cowardice or ill temper.

Your place in life is not fixed by heredity, nor are you condemned to the lower levels by circumstances or lack of opportunity. The Principle of Power is sufficient for all the requirements of your soul. No possible combination of circumstances can keep you down, if you make your personal attitude right and determine to rise. The power that formed you and purposed you for growth also controls the circumstances of society, industry, and government; and this power is never divided against itself. The power that is in you is in the things around you, and when you begin to move forward, the things will arrange themselves for your advantage. Growth is inherent in the development of humankind; all things external were designed to promote this growth. No sooner do we awaken our soul and enter on the advancing way than we find that not only is God for us, but nature, society, and other people are for us also. All things work together for our good if we obey the law. Poverty is no bar to greatness, for poverty can always be removed. Abraham Lincoln was a poor boy; George Stephenson, inventor of the locomotive engine, and one of the greatest of civil engineers, was a coal miner, working in a mine, when he awakened and began to think. James Watt was a sickly child, and was not strong enough to be sent to school. W. Clement Stone came from an impoverished family and as a child had to sell newspapers on the streets of Chicago to survive. But he overcame poverty and adversity to become a multimillionaire insurance executive. In each of these cases we see a Principle of Power that lifts a person above all opposition and negativity.

There is a Principle of Power in you. If you use it and apply it in a certain way you can overcome all heredity, and master all circumstances and conditions and become a great and powerful personality.

Chapter

3

THE SOURCE OF POWER

Our brain, body, mind, faculties, and talents are the mere instruments we use in demonstrating greatness. In themselves they do not make us great. We may have a large brain and a good mind, strong faculties, and brilliant talents, and yet may not be a great person unless we use all these in a great way. That quality which enables us to use our abilities in a great way makes us great; and to that quality we give the name of *wisdom*. Wisdom is the essential basis of greatness.

Wisdom is the power to perceive the best ends to aim at and the best means for reaching those ends. It *is* the power to perceive the right thing to do. The person who is wise enough to know the right thing to do, who is good enough to wish to do only the right thing and who is able and strong enough to do the right thing is a truly great person, who will instantly become marked as a personality of power in any community and will be respected and honored by all.

Wisdom is dependent upon knowledge. Where there is complete ignorance there can be no wisdom, no knowledge of the right thing to do. Our knowledge is comparatively limited and so our wisdom must be small, unless we can connect our mind with knowledge greater than our own and draw from it by inspiration, the wisdom that our own limitations deny us. Our knowledge is limited and uncertain; therefore, we cannot have wisdom in ourselves alone.

Only God knows all truth; therefore, only God can have real wisdom or know the right thing to do at all times. However, we can receive wisdom from God. Here is an example: Abraham Lincoln had limited education, but he had the power to perceive truth. In Lincoln we see preeminently apparent the fact that real wisdom consists in knowing the right thing to do at all times and under all circumstances, in having the will to do the right thing, and in having talent and ability enough to be competent and able to do the right thing. Back in the days of the abolition agitation, and during the compromise period, when most people were more or less confused as to what was right or as to what ought to be done, Lincoln was never uncertain. He saw through the superficial arguments of the pro-slavery adherents and he also saw the impracticability and fanaticism of the abolitionists. He saw the right ends to aim at and he saw the best means to attain those ends. It was because the citizens recognized that he perceived truth and knew the right thing to do that they made him president.

People who develop the power to perceive the truth, and who can show that they always know the right thing to do and that they can be trusted to do the right thing, will be honored and advanced; the whole world is looking eagerly for such leaders.

When Lincoln became president, he was surrounded by a multitude of so-called able advisers, hardly any two of whom were agreed. At times they were all opposed to his policies. At times almost the whole North was opposed to what he proposed to do. But he saw the truth when others were misled by appearances; his judgment was seldom or never wrong. He was at once the ablest statesman and the best soldier of the period. Where did he, a comparatively unlearned man, get this wisdom? It was not due to some fineness of texture of his brain. It was not due to some physical characteristic. It was not even a quality of mind due to superior reasoning power. Knowledge of truth is not often reached by the processes of reason. It was due to a spiritual insight. He perceived truth, but where did he perceive it and whence did the perception come?

We see something similar in George Washington, whose faith and courage, due to his perception of truth, held the colonies together during the long and often apparently hopeless struggle of the Revolution. We see the same thing in all great men and women. They perceive truth; but truth cannot be perceived until it exists; and there can be no truth until there is a mind to perceive it. Truth does not, exist apart from mind. Washington and Lincoln were in touch and communication with a mind that knew all knowledge and contained all truth – so have all who manifest wisdom. *Wisdom is obtained by reading the mind of God.*

One of the truly great men of all ages was Benjamin Franklin. He achieved greatness in several areas: his inventions such as the lightening rod and Franklin stove, his writings *Poor Richard's Almanac* and his autobiography, his contributions to America: as inspirer of both the Declaration of Independence and the Constitutions, his diplomacy, as ambassador to France, he negotiated the alliance which helped American win the Revolution.

He lived almost universally admired and died almost universally lamented. If he enjoyed life more than any other person at his time, it can also be said with truth that he contributed as much as any person of his time to the enjoyment of others.

He was tolerant of everything but intolerance, and made some charitable allowance even for that. We see him at different times of his life associating on friendly terms with Quakers, Moravians, Methodists, Presbyterians, Catholics, Deists, Jews and atheists meeting them on the common ground of human fellowship, making light of their theoretical opinions, valuing them only for their human worth.

This was because he did not overestimate human intellect nor undervalue the human heart. He was also aware that the strongholds of superstition are never to be carried by direct assault but gradually undermined by the rising tide of knowledge and good feeling. His whole life was a calm, good-natured protest against narrowness, intolerance and bigotry. He lived by the premise that the acceptable way of serving God is do good to His other creatures.

Chapter

4

PREPARATION

'Draw nigh to God and He will draw nigh to you.' If you become like God you can read His thoughts, and if you do not you will find the inspirational perception of truth impossible. You can never become a great man or woman until you have overcome anxiety, worry, and fear. It is impossible for an anxious person, a worried one, or a fearful one to perceive truth. All things are distorted and thrown out of their proper relations by such mental states and those who are in them cannot read the thoughts of God.

If you are poor, or if you are anxious about business or financial matters, you are recommended to study carefully the first part of this book, *The Science of Getting Rich.* That will present to you a solution for your problems of this nature, no matter how large or how complicated they may seem to be. There is not the least cause for worry about financial affairs. Every person who wills to do so may rise above want, and become rich. The same source upon which you propose to draw for mental development and spiritual power is at your service for the supply of all your material wants. Study this truth until it is fixed in your thoughts and until anxiety is banished from your mind; enter the Certain Way, which leads to material riches.

Perhaps you are worried about your health. It is possible for you to attain perfect health so that you may have strength sufficient for all that you wish to do and more. That Intelligence which stands ready to give you wealth and mental and spiritual power will rejoice to give you health also. Perfect health is yours for the asking, if you will only obey the simple laws of life and live right. Conquer ill health and cast out fear.

But it is not enough to rise above financial and physical anxiety and worry; you must rise above moral evil-doing as well. Sound your inner consciousness now for the motives that actuate you and make sure they are right. You must cast out lust, and cease to be ruled by appetite, and you must begin to govern appetite. You must eat only to satisfy hunger, never for gluttonous pleasure, and in all things you must make the flesh obey the spirit.

You must lay aside greed; have no unworthy motive in your desire to become rich and powerful. It is legitimate and right to desire riches, if you want them for the sake of the soul, but not if you desire them for the lusts of the flesh.

Cast out pride and vanity. Have no thought of trying to rule over others or of outdoing them. This is a vital point; there is no temptation so insidious as the selfish desire to rule over others. Do not envy others. You can have all that you want, and you need not envy any person what he or she has. Do not hold malice or enmity toward anyone; to do so cuts you off from the mind whose treasures you to seek to make your own. Lay aside all narrow personal ambition – and determine to seek the highest good aid to be swayed by no unworthy selfishness.

Go over all the foregoing and set these moral temptations out of your heart one by one. Determine to keep them out. Then resolve that you will not only abandon all evil thought but that you will forsake all deeds, habits, and courses of action which do not commend themselves to your noblest ideals. This is supremely important; make this resolution with all the power of your soul, and you are ready for the next step toward greatness, which will be explained in the following chapter.

Chapter

5

The Social Point of View

'*Without faith it is impossible to please God,*' and without faith it is impossible for you to become great. The distinguishing characteristic of all really great men and women is an unwavering faith. We see this in Lincoln during the dark days of the Civil War. We see it in Washington at Valley Forge. We see it in Livingstone, the crippled missionary, threading the mazes of Africa, his soul aflame with the determination to let in the light upon the accursed slave trade, which his soul abhorred. We see it in Mahatma Gandhi, Clara Barton, Martin Luther King, in every man and woman who has attained a place on the muster roll of the great ones of the world.

Faith – not a faith in one's self or in one's own powers but faith in principle – in the Something Great which upholds right, and which may be relied upon to give us the victory in due time. Without this faith it is not possible for anyone to rise to real greatness. Whether you have this faith or not depends upon your point of view. You must learn to see the world as being produced by evolution – as a something that is evolving and becoming, not as a finished work. Millions of years ago God worked with very low and crude forms of life; low and crude, yet each perfect after its kind.

Higher and more complex organisms, animal and vegetable, appeared through the successive ages. The earth passed through stage after stage in its development, each stage perfect in itself, and to be succeeded by a higher one. Note that the so-called 'lower organisms' are as perfect after their kind as the higher ones; that the world in the Eocene period was perfect for that period. It was perfect; but God's work was not finished. This is true of the world today. Physically, socially, and industrially it is all good, and it is all perfect. It is not complete anywhere or in any part, but as far as the handiwork of God has gone it is perfect.

This must be your point of view. That the world and all it contains is perfect, though not completed.

'All's right with the world.' That is the great fact. There is nothing wrong with anything; there is nothing wrong with anybody. All the facts of life must be contemplated from this standpoint. There is nothing wrong with nature. Nature is a great advancing presence, working beneficently for the happiness of all. All things in Nature are good; it has no evil. It is not complete, for creation is still unfinished, but it is going on to give us even more bountifully than it has given to us in the past. Nature is a partial expression of God, and God is love. Nature is perfect but not complete.

This is also true of human society and government. Yes, we still have monopolies and cartels and strikes and lockouts and so on. All these things are part of the forward movement; they are incidental to the evolutionary process of completing society. When it is complete there will be no more of these discords; but it cannot be completed without them. Look at society, government, and industry as being perfect now, but not yet complete. However, you must recognize that it is advancing rapidly toward being complete, and then you will understand that there is nothing to fear, no cause for anxiety, nothing to worry about. Never complain of any of these things. They are perfect; this is the very best possible world for the stage of development we have reached. It is a stage of development that we are moving through on our way to a better life.

The people make society what it is, and as the people rise above the bestial thought, society will rise above the beastly in its manifestations.

All this does not prevent you from working for better things. You can work to complete an unfinished society, instead of to renovate a decaying one; and you can work with a better heart and a more hopeful spirit. It will make an immense difference with your faith and spirit whether you look upon civilization as a good thing that is becoming better or as a bad and evil thing that is decaying. One viewpoint gives you an advancing and expanding mind and the other gives you a descending and decreasing mind. One viewpoint will make you grow greater and the other will inevitably cause you to grow smaller. One will enable you to work for the eternal things; to do large works in a great way toward the completing of all that is incomplete and inharmonious. The other will make you a mere patchwork reformer, working almost without hope to save a few lost souls from what you will grow to consider a lost and doomed world. So you see it makes a vast difference to you, this matter of the social viewpoint. 'All's right with the world. Nothing can possibly be wrong but my personal attitude, and I will make that right. I will see the facts of nature and all the events, circumstances, and conditions of society, politics, government, and industry from the highest viewpoint. It is all perfect, though incomplete. It is all the handiwork of God; behold, it is all very good.'

Chapter

6

THE INDIVIDUAL POINT OF VIEW

Important as the matter of your point of view for the facts of social life is, it is of less moment than your viewpoint for others, for your acquaintances, friends, relatives, your immediate family, and, most of all, yourself. You must learn not to look upon the world as a lost and decaying thing but as a something perfect and glorious that is going on to a most beautiful completeness. You must learn to see men and women not as lost and accursed things, but as perfect beings advancing to become complete. There are no 'bad' or 'evil' people. An engine that is on the rails pulling a heavy train is perfect after its kind, and it is good. The power of steam that drives it is good. Let a broken rail throw the engine into the ditch, and it does not become bad or evil by being so displaced – it is a perfectly good engine, but off the track. The power of steam that drives it into the ditch and wrecks it is not evil, but a perfectly good power. So that which is misplaced or applied in an incomplete or partial way is not evil. There are no evil people. There are perfectly good people who are off the track, but they do not need condemnation or punishment; they only need to get upon the rails again.

That which is undeveloped or incomplete often appears to us as evil because of the way we have trained ourselves to think. The root of a bulb that shall produce a white lily is an unsightly thing; one might look upon it with disgust, but how foolish we should be to condemn the bulb for its appearance when we know the lily is within it. The root is perfect after its kind; it is a perfect but an incomplete lily, and so we must learn to look upon every man and woman no matter how unlovely in outward manifestation; they are perfect in their stage of being and they are becoming complete. Behold, it is all very good.

Once we come into a comprehension of this fact and arrive at this point of view, we lose all desire to find fault with people, to judge them, criticize them, or condemn them. We no longer work as those who are saving lost souls, but as those who are among the angels, working out the completion of a glorious heaven. We are born of the spirit and we see the kingdom of God. We no longer see ourselves as trees walking, but our vision is complete. We have nothing but good words to say. It is all good; a great and glorious humanity coming to completeness. And in our association with others this puts us into an expansive and enlarging attitude of mind. We see them as great beings and we begin to deal with them and their affairs in a great way. But if we fall to the other point of view and see a lost and degenerate race we shrink into the contracting mind, and our dealings with men and their affairs will be in a small and contracted way. Remember to hold steadily to this point of view. If you do you cannot fail to begin at once to deal with your acquaintances and neighbors and with your own family as a great personality deals with others. This same viewpoint must be the one from which you regard yourself. You must always see yourself as a great advancing soul.

Learn to say: 'There is *that* in me of which I am made, which knows no imperfection, weakness, or sickness. The world is incomplete, *but God in my own consciousness is both perfect and complete.* Nothing can be wrong but my own personal attitude, and my own personal attitude can be wrong only when I disobey *that* which is within. I am a perfect manifestation of God so far as I have gone, and I will press on to be complete. I trust and not be afraid.'

When you are able to say this understandingly you will have lost all fear and you will be far advanced upon the road to the development of a great and powerful personality.

Chapter

7

CONSECRATION

Having attained to the viewpoint that puts you into the right relations with the world and with other people, the next step is consecration. *Consecration in its true sense simply means obedience to the soul.* You have that within you that is ever impelling you toward the upward and advancing way; and that impelling something is the divine Principle of Power. You must obey it without question. No one will deny the statement that if you are to be great, the greatness must-be a manifestation of something within. You cannot question that this something must be the very greatest and highest that is within. It is not the mind, or the intellect, or the reason.

You cannot be great if you go no farther back for principle than to your reasoning power. Reason knows neither principle nor morality. Your reason is like a lawyer in that it will argue for either side. The intellect of a thief will plan robbery and murder as readily as the intellect of a saint will plan a great philanthropy. Intellect helps us to see the best means and manner of doing the right thing, but intellect never shows us the right thing. Intellect and reason serve selfish people for their selfish ends as readily as they serve unselfish people for their unselfish ends. Use intellect and reason without regard to principle, and you may, become known as a very able person, but you will never become known as a person whose life shows the power of real greatness. There is too much training of the intellect and reasoning powers and too little training in obedience to the soul. This is the only thing that can be wrong with your personal attitude – when it fails to be one of obedience to the Principle of Power.

By going back to your own center you can always find the pure idea of right for every relationship. To be great and to have power it is only necessary to conform your life to the pure idea as you find it in your conscience. Every compromise on this point is made at the expense of a loss of power. This you *must* remember.

There are many ideas in your mind that you have outgrown, and which, from force of habit, you still permit to dictate the actions of your life. Cease all this; abandon everything you have outgrown. There are many ignoble customs – social and other, which you still follow, although you know they tend to dwarf and belittle you and keep you acting in a small way. Rise above all this. This does not mean that you should absolutely disregard conventionalities, or the commonly accepted standards of right and wrong. You cannot do this, but you can deliver your soul from most of the narrow restrictions that bind so many people. Do not give your time and strength to the support of obsolete institutions, religious or otherwise; do not be bound by creeds in which you do not believe. *Be free.* You have perhaps formed some sensual habits of mind or body; abandon them. You still indulge in distrustful fears that things will go wrong, or that people will betray you, or mistreat you; get above all of them. You still act selfishly in many ways and on many occasions; cease to do so. Abandon all these, and in place of them put the best actions you can form a conception of in your mind. If you desire to advance, and you are not doing so remember that it can be only because your thought is better than your practice. You must do as well as you think.

Let your thoughts be ruled by principle, and then live up to your thoughts.

Let your attitude in business, in politics, in neighborhood affairs, and in your own home be the expression of the best thoughts you can think. Let your manner toward all men and women, great and small, and especially to your own family circle, always be the most kindly, gracious, and courteous you can picture in your imagination. Remember your viewpoint; you are a god in the company of gods and must conduct yourself accordingly.

Winston Churchill was a person fully consecrated to his ideals. He was a persistent advocate of conciliation. He shunned the paths of division and unnecessary confrontation. In international affairs he consistently sought the settlement of grievances of those who had been defeated and the building up of meaningful associations for the reconciliation of former enemies. After two world wars he argued in favor of maintaining the strength of the victors in order to redress the grievances of the vanquished and to preserve the peace. It was he who first used the word 'summit' for a meeting of the leaders of the western and communist worlds, and did the utmost to set up meetings to end the dangerous confrontations of the cold war.

A perceptive and shrewd commentator on the events taking place around him, Churchill was always an advocate of bold, farsighted courses of action. One of his greatest gifts, seen in his several thousand public speeches, as well as heard in his many broadcasts, was his ability to use his exceptional mastery of words and love of language, to convey detailed arguments and essential truths; to inform, to convince, and to inspire. He was a man of great humor and warmth and magnanimity. His dislike of unfairness, of victimization, and of bullying—whether at home or abroad—was the foundation of much of his thinking. His finest hour was the leadership of Britain when it was most isolated, most threatened and most weak, when his own courage, determination, consecration and belief in democracy became one with the nation.

The steps to complete consecration are few and simple. You cannot be ruled from below if you are to be great; you must rule from above. Therefore, you cannot be governed by physical impulses; you must bring your body into subjection to the mind; but your mind, without principle, may lead you into selfishness and immoral ways. You must say to yourself:

'I surrender my body to be ruled by my mind; I surrender my mind to be governed by my soul, and I surrender my soul to the guidance of God.'

Make this consecration complete and thorough, and you have taken the second great step in the way of greatness and power.

Chapter

8

IDENTIFICATION

Having recognized God as the advancing presence in nature, society, and humankind, and harmonized yourself with all these, and having consecrated yourself to that within you that impels toward the greatest and the highest, the next step is to become aware of and recognize fully the fact that the Principle of Power within you is God Himself. You must consciously identify yourself with the Highest. This is not some false or untrue position to be assumed; it is a fact to be recognized. You are already one with God; you want to become consciously aware of it.

God has given humankind the principle of power. This is not limited to a few exceptional people, but to all of us. The Principle of Power is in within each of us, but our consciousness is limited. We do not know all there is to know and so we are liable to error and mistake. To save ourselves from these we must unite our minds to that outside ourselves that does know all. We must become consciously one with God.

There is a mind surrounding us on every side, closer than breathing, nearer than hands and feet, and in this mind is the memory of all that has ever happened, from the greatest convulsions of nature in prehistoric days to the fall of a sparrow in this present time – all that is in existence now as well. Held in this Mind is the great purpose that is behind all nature, and so it knows what is going to be. We are surrounded by a Mind that knows all there is to know, past, present, and to come. Everything that humans have said or done or written is present there. We are of one identical stuff with this Mind.

Your identification of yourself with the Infinite must be accomplished by conscious recognition on your part. Recognizing it as a fact, that there is only God, and that all intelligence is in the one substance. You must truly believe in the Infinite God and surrender yourself to conscious unity with Him.

If you have been thorough in the work as outlined in the preceding chapters; if you have attained to the true viewpoint, and if your consecration is complete, you will not find conscious identification hard to attain; and once it is attained, the power you seek is yours, for you have made yourself one with all the power there is.

Chapter

9

IDEALIZATION

A key step in setting the stage for greatness is to think of yourself as you desire to be, and set your ideal as near to perfection as your imagination is capable of forming the conception. This is called a 'thought-form.' For example, if a young law student wishes to become great, let him picture himself (while attending to the viewpoint, consecration, and identification, as previously directed) as a great lawyer, pleading his case with matchless eloquence and power before the judge and jury; as having an unlimited command of truth, of knowledge, and of wisdom. Let him picture himself as the great lawyer in every possible situation and contingency. While he is still only the student in all circumstances, let him never forget or fail to be the great lawyer in his thought-form of himself. As the thought-form grows more definite and habitual in his mind, the creative energies, both within and without, are set at work. He begins to manifest the form from within and all the essentials without, which go into the picture, begin to be impelled toward him. He makes himself into the image and God works with him. Nothing can prevent him from becoming what he wishes to be.

In the same general way the musical student pictures herself as performing perfect harmonies, and as delighting vast audiences; the actor forms the highest conception he is capable of in regard to his art, and applies this conception to himself.

The sales representative and the mechanic do exactly the same thing. Fix upon your ideal of what you wish to make of yourself; consider well and be sure that you make the right choice; that is, the one that will be the most satisfactory to you in a general way. Do not pay too much attention to the advice or suggestions of those around you; do not believe that anyone can know, better than yourself, what is right for you. Listen to what others have to say, but always form your own conclusions. *Do not let other people decide what you are to be. Be what you feel that you want to be.*

Do not be misled by a false notion of obligation or duty. You can owe no possible obligation or duty to others, which should prevent you from making the most of yourself. Be true to yourself, and you cannot then be false to anyone. When you have fully decided what thing you want to be, form the highest conception of that thing that you are capable of imagining, and make that conception a thought-form. Hold that thought-form as a fact, as the real truth about yourself, and believe in it. Close your ears to all adverse suggestions. Never mind if people call you a fool and a dreamer. Dream on.

Remember that Bonaparte, the half-starved lieutenant, always saw himself as the general of armies and the master of France, and he became in outward realization what he held himself to be in mind. So likewise will you. Attend carefully to all that has been said in the preceding chapters, and act as directed in the following ones, and you'll become what you want to be.

Michael Jordan is another person who early in his life saw himself as a great athlete and he planned every step of the way to become one of the greatest athletes of his generation. He always had the determination to win and the will power to do all that must be done to keep in shape and play his very best. He is committed to maintain high standards and to keep improving his own records. Jordan learned this lesson early. In high school, he was dropped from the team, but his determination to be reinstated led to his starting a heavy regimen of practice daily – which he still follows. He takes each doubt as a challenge, and each year he's had a new incentive. When he returned to basketball after a few years away from the game, his critics said that he was past his prime and that he was slower and couldn't win another championship. He took this as a challenge and it just honed his determination to show them they were wrong. He worked harder than ever to improve and maintain his conditioning. He designed a year-round conditioning program with his own personal trainer and his own gym and weight room He recognized that as one grows older, the body starts giving signals that you must listen to and do the things that are correct in order to stay in the best shape possible to consistently play championship. The results were astounding. Jordan led his team to the championship in 1996 and 1997 and in both years was named the Most Valuable Player. Michael Jordan's determination to achieve his goals is a lesson to all of us that if we are determined to achieve our goals, neither age nor skepticism of others can deter us. But determination is only the first step. It must be followed by hard work, a regimen of physical and mental exercise and whatever it takes to bring us to peak performance.

Chapter

10

REALIZATION

If you were to stop with the close of the last chapter, you would never become great; you would be indeed a mere dreamer of dreams, a castle-builder. Too many do stop there; they do not understand the necessity for present action in realizing the vision and bringing the thought-form into manifestation.

Two things are necessary: first, the making of the thought-form, and, second, the actual appropriation to yourself of all that goes into and around the thought-form. When you have made your thought-form, you are already *internally* what you want to be. Next you must become *externally* what you want to be. You are already great within, but you are not yet actually doing the great things. You cannot begin, on the instant, to do the great things; you cannot be before the world the great actor, or lawyer, or musician, or personality you know yourself to be; no one will entrust great things to you as yet for you have not made yourself known. But you can always begin to do small things in a great way.

Here lies the whole secret. You can begin to be great today in your own home, in your store or office, on the street, everywhere; you can begin to make yourself known as great, and you can do this by doing everything you do in a great way. You must put the whole power of your great soul into every act, however small and commonplace, and so reveal to your family, your friends, and neighbors what you really are. Do not brag or boast of yourself; do not go about telling people what a great personage you are. *Simply live in a great way.* No one will believe you if you tell him you are a great man or woman, but no one can doubt your greatness if you show it in your actions. In your domestic circle be so just, so generous, so courteous, and kindly that your family, your wife, husband, children, brothers, and sisters shall know that you are a great and noble soul. In all your relations with others be great, just, generous, courteous, and kindly. The great are never otherwise.

Next, and most important, you must have absolute faith in your own perceptions of truth. Never act in haste or hurry. Be deliberate in everything; wait until you feel that you know the true way. And when you do feel that you know the true way, be guided by your own faith though all the world shall disagree with you. If you do not believe what God tells you in little things, you will never draw upon His wisdom and knowledge in larger things.

When you feel deeply that a certain act is the right act, do it and have perfect faith that the consequences will be good. When you are deeply impressed that a certain thing *is* true, no matter what the appearances to the contrary may be, accept that thing as true and act accordingly. The one way to develop a perception of truth in large things is to trust absolutely to your present perception of truth in small things. Remember that you are seeking to develop this very power or faculty – the perception of truth. You are learning to read the thoughts of God. Nothing is great and nothing is small in the sight of Omnipotence. God holds the sun in its place, but He also notes a sparrow's fall, and numbers the hairs of your head. God is as much interested in the little matters of everyday life as He is in the affairs of nations. You can perceive truth about family and neighborhood affairs as well as about matters of statecraft. And the way to begin is to have perfect faith in the truth in these small matters, as it is revealed to you from day to day. When you feel deeply impelled to take a course that seems contrary to all reason and worldly judgment, take that course. Listen to the suggestions and advice of others, but always do what you feel deeply within you to be the true thing to do. Rely with absolute faith, at all times, on your own perception of truth; but be sure that you listen to God — that you do not act in haste, fear, or anxiety.

Rely upon your perception of truth in all the facts and circumstances of life. If you feel sure of the truth of any circumstance or happening, near or distant, past, present or to come, trust in your perception. You may make occasional mistakes at first because of your imperfect understanding of the perception. You will soon be guided so that you are almost invariably right. Soon your family and friends will begin to defer, more and more, to your judgment and to be guided by you. Soon your neighbors and townsmen will be coming to you for counsel and advice; soon you will be recognized as one who is great in small things, and you will be called upon more and more to take charge of larger things. All that is necessary is to be guided absolutely, in all things by your inner light, by your perception of truth. Obey your soul, have perfect faith in yourself. Never think of yourself with doubt or distrust, or as one who makes mistakes.

A modern example of a person who had confidence in the rightness of his ideas is Fred Smith, the founder of Federal Express (FEDEX). When Smith was a student in an economics class at Yale University, his professor stated that airfreight was the wave of the future and would be the primary source of revenue for the airlines. Smith wrote a paper disagreeing. His argument was that the passenger route patterns that were the primary airline routes were wrong for freight. He noted that because costs would not come down with volume, the only way airfreight could be profitable was through a whole new system that would reach out to smaller cities as well as big ones and be designed for packages, not people. The professor considered this entirely unfeasible and gave Smith's paper a low grade.

Smith's concept was to start an all-freight airline that would fly primarily at night when the airports weren't congested. It would carry small, high-priority packages when speed of delivery was more important than cost. It would bring all the packages to a central point (He chose his home town – Memphis) where, through a specially designed computer program, the packages would be sorted, dispersed and loaded on airplanes that were flown to the ultimate destinations. By consolidating all shipments to smaller cities, it would enable the company to fly full planeloads to cities all over the country and eventually the world.

Smith believed that venture capitalists would be interested and excited about this innovative idea. But to his shock, little interest was developed in the financial community. This did not stop Smith. As a result of his enthusiasm for the project and because he had the courage of his convictions, he raised $91 million to finance his untested idea.

At this point the competing carriers realized that Smith's concept was a potential threat to their industry. The major airlines tried to forestall this new competition by lobbying the Civil Aeronautics Board to refuse Smith the necessary permission. Smith's team found a loophole in the law. Planes with a payload under 7,500 pounds did not need CAB permission to operate.

Smith went ahead and assembled a fleet of small jets. He began construction of his main facility at Memphis and began servicing 75 airports. FEDEX would pick up packages at airports all over the country and fly them to Memphis, where they were sorted out and processed for immediate reshipment to other cities. Once unloaded, FEDEX trucks delivered them to their destinations. Smith set a goal to get all packages to their destinations within 24 hours of its pick-up – and this goal was almost always met.

Despite the hard work and efforts of the company, the first few years were financial disasters. Losses amounted to millions of dollars. The investors were seriously concerned. Federal was falling far short of Smith's projections. Despite the losses, which the investors blamed on Smith, and even talk of removing him and taking over the company, Smith did not lose faith. His courage never faltered. He hired experts and worked day and night with them to solve operational problems. His resulted in Federal's revenues reaching $75 million in the next fiscal year, with a profit of $3.6 million.

Chapter
11

HURRY AND HABIT

No doubt you have many problems, domestic, social, physical, and financial, which seem to you to be pressing for instant solution. You have debts that must be paid, or other obligations that must be met; you are unhappily or inharmoniously placed, and feel that something must be done at once. Do not get into a hurry and act from superficial impulses. You can trust God for the solution of all your personal riddles. There is no hurry. There is only God, and all is well with the world.

There is an invincible power in you, and the same power is in the things you want. It is bringing them to you and bringing you to them. This is a thought that you must grasp, and hold continuously that the same intelligence that is in you is in the things you desire. They are impelled toward you as strongly and decidedly as your desire impels you toward them. The tendency, therefore, of a steadily held thought must be to bring the things you desire to you and to group them around you. So long as you hold your thought and your faith right all must go well. *Nothing can be wrong but your own personal attitude, and that will not be wrong if you trust and are not afraid.*

Hurry is a manifestation of fear. One who does not fear has plenty of time. If you act with perfect faith in your own perceptions of truth, you will never be too late or too early and nothing will go wrong. If things appear to be going wrong, do not get disturbed; it is only in appearance. Nothing can go wrong in this world but yourself.

You can go wrong only by getting into the wrong mental attitude. Whenever you find yourself getting excited, worried, or into the mental attitude of hurry, sit down and think it over. Play a game of some kind, or take a vacation. Go on a trip, and all will be right when you return. As surely as you find yourself in the mental attitude of haste, just as surely may you know that you are out of the mental attitude of greatness. Hurry and fear will instantly cut your connection with the universal mind; you will get no power, no wisdom, and no information until you are calm. And to fall into the attitude of hurry will check the action of the Principle of Power within you. Fear turns strength to weakness.

Remember that poise and power are inseparably associated. The calm and balanced mind is the strong and great mind; the hurried and agitated mind is the weak one. Whenever you fall into the mental state of hurry you may know that you have lost the right viewpoint; you are beginning to look upon the world, or some part of it, as going wrong. Consider the fact that this world is perfect, now, with all that it contains. Nothing is going wrong; nothing can be wrong; be poised, be calm, be cheerful; have faith in God.

Next, examine your habits. It is probable that your greatest difficulty will be to overcome your old habitual ways of thought, and to form new habits. The world is ruled by habit. Dictators, tyrants, masters, and plutocrats hold their positions solely because the people have come to habitually accept them. Things are as they are only because people have formed the habit of accepting them as they are. When the people change their habitual thought about governmental, social, and industrial institutions, they will change the institutions. Habit rules us all.

You have formed, perhaps, the habit of thinking of yourself as a common person, as one of a limited ability, or as being more or less of a failure. Whatever you habitually think yourself to be, that you are. You must form, now, a greater and better habit; you must form a conception of yourself as a being of limitless power, and habitually think that you are that being. It is the habitual, not the periodical thought that decides your destiny. It will avail you nothing to sit apart for a few moments several times a day to affirm that you are great, if during all the balance of the day, while you are about your regular vocation, you think of yourself as not great. No amount of praying or affirmation will make you great if you still habitually regard yourself as being small.

The use of prayer and affirmation is to change your habit of thought. Any act, mental or physical often repeated, becomes a habit. The purpose of mental exercises is to repeat certain thoughts over and over until the thinking of those thoughts becomes constant and habitual. The thoughts we continually repeat become convictions. What you must do is to repeat the new thought of yourself until it is the only way in which you think of yourself. Habitual thought, and not environment or circumstance has made you what you are. We all have some central idea or thought-form of ourselves, and by this idea we classify and arranges all our facts and external relationships. You are classifying your facts either according to the idea that you are a great and strong personality, or according to the idea that you are limited, common, or weak. If the latter is the case you must change your central idea. Get a new mental picture of yourself. Do not try to become great by repeating mere strings of words or superficial formula; but repeat over and over the *thought* of your own power and ability until you classify external facts, and decide your place everywhere by this idea.

Chapter

12

THOUGHT

Greatness is attained only by the thinking of great thoughts. We can never become great in outward personality unless we are great internally; and we cannot be great internally until we *think*. No amount of education, reading, or study can make you great without thought; but thought can make you great with very little study. There are altogether too many people who are trying to make something of themselves by reading books without thinking. All such will fail. You are not mentally developed by what you read, but by what you think about what you read.

Thinking is the hardest and most exhausting of all labor and hence many people shrink from it. God has so formed us that we are continuously impelled to thought. We must either think or engage in some activity to escape thought. The headlong, continuous chase for pleasure in which most people spend all their leisure time is only an effort to escape thought. If they are alone, or if they have nothing amusing to take their attention, as a novel to read or a show to see, they must think; and to escape from thinking they resort to novels, televisions sit-coms, and all the endless devices of the purveyors of amusement. Most people spend the greater part of their leisure time running away from thought, hence they are where they are. We never move forward until we begin to think.

Thinking, not mere knowledge or information makes personality. Thinking is growth; you cannot think without growing. Every thought engenders another thought. Write one idea and others will follow until you have written a page. You cannot fathom your own mind; it has neither bottom nor boundaries. Your first thoughts may be crude, but as you go on thinking you will use more and more of yourself; you will quicken new brain cells into activity and you will develop new faculties. Heredity, environment, circumstances – all things must give way before you if you practice sustained and continuous thought. But, on the other hand, if you neglect to think for yourself and only use other people's thought, you will never know what you are capable of, and you will end by being incapable of anything.

There can be no real greatness without original thought. All that we do outwardly is the expression and completion of our inward thinking. No action is possible without thought, and no great action is possible until a great thought has preceded it. Action is the second form of thought, and personality is the materialization of thought. Environment is the result of thought; things group themselves or arrange themselves around you according to your thought. There is some central idea or conception of yourself by which all the facts of your life are arranged and classified. Change this central idea and you change the arrangement or classification of all the facts and circumstances of your life. You are what you are because you think as you do. You are where you are because you think as you do.

You see then the immense importance of thinking about the great essentials set forth in the preceding chapters. You must not accept them in any superficial way; you must think about them until they are a part of your central idea. Go back to the matter of the point of view and consider, in all its bearings, the tremendous thought that you live in a perfect world among perfect people, and that nothing can possibly be wrong with you but your own personal attitude. Think about all this until you fully realize all that it means to you. Consider that this is God's world and that it is the best of all possible worlds; that He has brought it thus far toward completion by the processes of organic, social, and industrial evolution, and that it is going on to greater completeness and harmony. Consider that there is one great, perfect, intelligent Principle of Life and Power, causing all the changing phenomena of the cosmos. Think about all this until you see that it is true, and until you comprehend how you should live and act as a citizen of such a perfect whole.

Next, think of the wonderful truth that this great Intelligence is in you. It is your own intelligence. It is an Inner Light impelling you toward the right thing and the best thing, the greatest act, and the highest happiness. It is a Principle of Power in you, giving you all the ability and genius there is. It will infallibly guide you to the best if you will submit to it and walk in the light. Consider what is meant by your consecration of yourself when you say, "I will obey my soul." This is a sentence of tremendous meaning; it must revolutionize the attitude and behavior of the average person.

Henry Ford was one of the great innovators of modern times. Not only did he make it possible for most everyone to own an automobile, but by making the most of the intelligence God gave him, he revolutionized the entire system of manufacturing by introducing the mass production system.

Just as Ford revolutionized manufacturing, Steve Jobs revolutionized the computer industry. When he founded Apple Computer, his idea to create a personal computer that would be used by small businesses and by individuals in their homes. Most 'experts in the field' scoffed at this idea. After all, computers were too complex for any but technocrats to understand and operate. But Steve listened to his 'inner light' and persisted, opening a whole new vista in the computer field.

Chapter

13

ACTION AT HOME

Do not merely think that you are going to become great; think *that you are great now.* Do not think that you will begin to act in a great way at some future time; begin now. Do not think that you will act in a great way when you reach a different environment; act in a great way where you are now. Do not think that you will begin to act in a great way when you begin to deal with great things; begin to deal in a great way with small things. Do not think that you will begin to be great when you get among more intelligent people, or among people who understand you better; begin now to deal in a great way with the people around you.

If you are not in an environment where there is scope for your best powers and talents you can move in due time; but meanwhile you can be great where you are. Lincoln was as great when he was a backwoods lawyer as when he was President. As a backwoods lawyer he did common things in a great way, and that made him President. Had he waited until he reached Washington to begin to be great, he would have remained unknown. You are not made great by the location in which you happen to be, or by the things with which you may surround yourself. You are not made great by what you receive from others, and you can never manifest greatness so long as you depend on others. You will manifest greatness only when you begin to stand alone. Dismiss all thought of reliance on externals, whether things, books, or people. As Emerson said, 'Shakespeare will never be made by the study of Shakespeare.' Shakespeare will be made only by the thinking of Shakespearean thoughts.

Never mind how the people around you, including those of your own household, may treat you. That has nothing at all to do with your being great; that is, it cannot hinder you from being great. People may neglect you and be unthankful and unkind in their attitude toward you. Does that prevent you from being great in your manner and attitude toward them? Would God be great if He should go away and sulk because people were unthankful and did not appreciate Him? Treat the unthankful and the evil in a great and perfectly kind way, just as God does.

Do not talk about your greatness. You are really, in essential nature, no greater than those around you. You may have entered upon a way of living and thinking which they have not yet found, but they are perfect on their own plane of thought and action. You are entitled to no special honor or consideration for your greatness. You are a god, but you are among gods. You will fall into the boastful attitude if you see other people's shortcomings and failures and compare them with your own virtues and successes. If you fall into the boastful attitude of mind, you will cease to be great, and become small. Think of yourself as a perfect being among perfect beings, and meet every person as an equal, not as either a superior or an inferior. Give yourself no airs; great people never do. Ask no honors and seek for no recognition; honors and recognition will come fast enough if you are entitled to them.

Begin at home. It is a great person who can always be poised, assured, calm, and perfectly kind and considerate at home. If your manner and attitude in your own family are always the best you can think, you will soon become the one on whom all the others will rely. You will be a tower of strength and a support in time of trouble. You will be loved and appreciated. At the same time do not make the mistake of throwing yourself away in the service of others. Great people respect themselves; they serve and help, but are never slavishly servile. You cannot help your family by being a slave to them, or by doing for them those things that by right they should do for themselves. You do not help people when you wait on them too much. The selfish and exacting are a great deal better off if their exactions are denied. The ideal world is not one where there are a lot of people being waited on by other people. It is a world where all of us must wait on ourselves. Meet all demands, selfish and otherwise, with perfect kindness and consideration; but do not allow yourself to be made a slave to the whims, caprices, exactions, or slavish desires of any member of your family. To do so is not great, and it injures the other party.

Do not become uneasy over the failures or mistakes of any member of your family and feel that you must interfere. Do not be disturbed if others seem to be going wrong, and feel that you must step in and set them right. Remember that every person is perfect on his or her own plane. You cannot improve on the work of God. Do not meddle with the personal habits and practices of others, though they are your nearest and dearest; these things are none of your business. Nothing can be wrong but your own personal attitude; make that right and you will know that all else is right. You are a truly great soul when you can live with those who do things that you do not do, and yet refrain from either criticism or interference. Do the things that are right for you to do, and believe that all members of your family *are* doing the things that are right for them. Do not be enslaved by anyone else, but be just as careful that you do not enslave anyone else to your own notions of what is right.

Think, and think deeply and continuously; be perfect in your kindness and consideration. Let your attitude be that of a god among gods, and not that of a god among inferior beings. This is the way to be great in your own home.

Chapter

14

ACTION ABROAD

The rules that apply to your action at home must apply to your action everywhere. Never forget for an instant that this is a perfect world, and that you are a god among gods. You are as great as the greatest, but all are your equals.

Rely absolutely on your perception of truth. Trust to the inner light rather than to reason, but be sure that your perception comes from the inner light; act in poise and calmness; be still and attend on God. Your identification of yourself with the Eternal One will give you all the knowledge you need for guidance in any contingency that may arise in your own life or in the lives of others. It is only necessary that you should be supremely calm, and rely upon the eternal wisdom that is within you. If you act in poise and faith, your judgment will always be right, and you will always know exactly what to do. Do not hurry or worry. In the darkest days of World War II, when the Nazis had overrun Europe, when the Luftwaffe was bombing London every night, and when it appeared that England would be invaded at any moment, Winston Churchill stood before the nation and inspired them to remain steadfast, encouraged them to regain hope and revitalized them in their commitment to victory. This seemingly irreverent leader was truly a voice of God.

Have perfect faith in yourself and in your own ability to cope with any combination of circumstances that may arise. Do not be disturbed if you are alone; if you need friends they will be brought to you at the right time. Do not be disturbed if you feel that you are ignorant; the information that you need will be furnished you when it is time for you to have it. That which is in you impelling you forward is in the things and people you need, impelling them toward you. If there is a particular person you need to know, he or she will be introduced to you. If there is a particular book you need to read it will be placed in your hands at the right time. All the knowledge you need will come to you from both external and internal sources. Your information and your talents will always be equal to the requirements of the occasion. As soon as you awaken and begin to use your faculties in a great way you will apply power to the development of your brain; new cells will be created and dormant cells quickened into activity, and your brain will be qualified as a perfect instrument for your mind.

Do not try to do great things until you are ready to go about them in a great way. If you undertake to deal with great matters in a small way—that is, from a low viewpoint or with incomplete consecration and wavering faith and courage—you will fail. Do not be in a hurry to get to the great things. Doing great things will not make you great, but becoming great will certainly lead you to the doing of great things. Begin to be great where you are and in the things you do every day. Do not be in haste to be found out or recognized as a great personality. Do not be disappointed if you are not nominated for office within a month after you begin to practice what you read in this book. Great people never seek recognition or applause; they are not great because they want to be paid for being so. Greatness is reward enough for itself. The joy of being something and of knowing that you are advancing is the greatest of all joys possible.

If you begin in your own family, as described in the preceding chapter, and then assume the same mental attitude with your neighbors, friends, and those you meet in business, you will soon find that people are beginning to depend on you. Your advice will be sought, and a constantly increasing number of people will look to you for strength and inspiration, and rely upon your judgment. Here, as in the home, you must avoid meddling with other people's affairs. Help all who come to you, but do not go about officiously endeavoring to set other people right. Mind your own business. It is not part of your mission in life to correct people's morals, habits, or If you lead a great life and do not preach, you will save a thousand times as many souls as one who leads a small life and preaches continuously.

If you hold the right viewpoint of the world, others will find it out and be impressed by it through your daily conversation and practice. Do not try to convert others to your point of view, except by holding it and living accordingly. If your consecration is perfect you do not need to tell anyone; it will speedily become apparent to all that you are guided by a higher principle than the average man or woman. If your identification with God is complete, you do not need to explain the fact to others; it will become self-evident. To become known as a great personality, you have nothing to do but to live. Do not go hunting for big things to do. Live a great life where you are, and in the daily work you have to do, and greater works will surely find you out. Big things will come to you, asking to be done.

Be so impressed with the value of a person that you treat even a beggar or the tramp with the most distinguished consideration. All is God. Every man and woman is perfect. Let your manner be that of a god addressing other gods. However, do not save all your consideration for just the poor; the millionaire is as good as the tramp. This is a perfectly good world, and there is not a person or thing in it but is exactly right; be sure that you keep this in mind in dealing with all people.

Form your mental vision of yourself with care. Make the thought-form of yourself as you wish to be, and hold this with the faith that it is being realized, and with the purpose to realize it completely. Do every common act as a god should do it; speak every word as a god should speak it; meet men and women of both low and high estate as a god meets other divine beings. Begin acting in this way and continue acting in this way, and your development in ability and power will be great and rapid.

Chapter

15

SOME FURTHER EXPLANATIONS

One area that is vitally important is the matter of the point of view. It is the one that is likely to give the student the most trouble. Some of us have been trained, partly by mistaken religious teachers, to look upon the world as being like a wrecked ship, storm-driven upon a rocky coast; utter destruction is inevitable at the end, and the most that can be done is to rescue, perhaps, a few of the crew. This view teaches us to consider the world as essentially bad and growing worse; and to believe that existing discords and inharmonies must continue and intensify until the end. It robs us of hope for society, government, and humanity, and gives us a decreasing outlook and contracting mind.

This is all wrong. The world is not wrecked. It is like a magnificent ocean liner with the engines in place and the machinery in perfect order. The tanks are full of oil and the ship is amply provisioned for the cruise; there is no lack of any good thing. Every provision God could devise has been made for the safety, comfort, and happiness of the crew. Yet, the vessel is out on the high seas tacking hither and thither because no one has yet learned the right course to steer. We are learning to steer, and in due time we will come grandly into the harbor of perfect harmony.

The world is good and growing better. Existing discords and inharmonies are but the rolling of the ship incidental to our own imperfect steering; they will all be removed in due time. This view gives us an increasing outlook and an expanding mind; it enables us to think largely of society and of ourselves, and to do things in a great way.

Furthermore, we see that nothing can be wrong with such a world or with any part of it, including our own affairs. If it is all moving on toward completion, then it is not going wrong; and as our own personal affairs are a part of the whole, they are not going wrong. You and all that you are concerned with are moving on toward completeness. Nothing can check this forward movement but yourself; and you can only check it by assuming a mental attitude that is at cross purposes with the mind of God. You have nothing to keep right but yourself. If you keep yourself right, nothing can possibly go wrong with you, and there is nothing to fear. No business or other disaster can come upon you if your personal attitude is right, for you are a part of that which is increasing and advancing, and you must increase and advance with it.

Moreover, your thought-form will be mostly shaped according to your view of the cosmos. If you see the world as a lost and ruined thing, you will see yourself as a part of it, and as partaking of its sins and weaknesses. If your outlook for the world as a whole is hopeless, your outlook for yourself cannot be hopeful. If you see the world as declining toward its end, you cannot see yourself as advancing. Unless you think well of all the works of God you cannot really think well of yourself, and unless you think well of yourself, you can never become great.

Never forget that your place in life including your material environment is determined by the thought-form you habitually hold of yourself. When you make a thought-form of yourself you can hardly fail to form in your mind a corresponding environment. If you think of yourself as an incapable, inefficient person, you will think of yourself with poor or cheap surroundings. Unless you think well of yourself, you will be sure to picture yourself in a more or less poverty-stricken environment. These thoughts, habitually held, become invisible forms in your mind, and are with you continually. In due time by the regular action of the eternal creative energy, the invisible thought-forms take control of your mind, and you are surrounded by your own thoughts made into material things.

See nature as a great living and advancing presence, and see human society in exactly the same way. It is all one, coming from one source, and it is all good. You are made of the same stuff as God. All the constituents of God are parts of you. Every power that God has is a constituent of humankind. You can move forward as you see God doing. You have within yourself the source of every power.

Chapter
16

MORE ABOUT THOUGHT

Give place here to some further consideration of thought. You will never become great until your own thoughts make you great, and therefore it is of the first importance that you should *think*. You will never do great things in the external world until you think great things in the internal world; and you will never think great things until you think about *truth* – about the verities. To think great things you must be absolutely sincere. To be sincere you must know that your intentions are right. Insincere or false thinking is never great, however logical and brilliant it may be.

The first and most important step is to seek the truth about human relations, to know what you ought to be to other people, and what they ought to be to you. This brings you back to the search for a right viewpoint. You should study organic and social evolution. Read the works of great philosophers and when you read, *think*; think the whole matter over until you see the world in the right way. *Think* about what God is doing until you can *see* what He is doing.

Your next step is to think yourself into the right personal attitude. Your viewpoint tells you what the right attitude is, and obedience to the soul puts you into it. It is only by making a complete consecration of yourself to the highest that is within you that you can attain to sincere thinking. So long as you know you are selfish in your aims, or dishonest or crooked in any way in your intentions or practices, your thinking will be false and your thoughts will have no power.

Think about the way you are doing things; about all your intentions, purposes and practices, until you know that they are right. The fact of your own complete unity with God is one that you cannot grasp without deep and sustained thinking. Anyone can accept the proposition in a superficial way, but to feel and realize a vital comprehension of it is another matter. It is easy to think of going *outside* of yourself to meet God, but it is not so easy to think of going *inside* yourself to meet God. But God is there, and in the holy of holies of your own soul you may meet Him face to face. It is a tremendous thing, this fact that all you need is already within you; that you do not have to consider how to get the power to do what you want to do or to make yourself what you want to be. You have only to consider how to use the power you have in the right way. And there is nothing to do but to begin. Use your perception of truth; you can see some truth today. Live fully up to that and you will see more truth tomorrow.

To rid yourself of the old false ideas you will have to think a great deal about the value of humankind, and the greatness and worth of a human soul. You must cease from looking at human mistakes and look at successes. Cease from seeing faults and see virtues. You can no longer look upon men and women as lost and ruined beings who are descending into hell; you must come to regard them as shining souls who are ascending toward heaven. It will require some exercise of will power to do this, but this is the legitimate use of the will—to decide what you will think about and how you will think. The function of the will is to direct thought. Think about the good side of people, the lovely, attractive part, and exert your will in refusing to think of anything else in connection with them.

Let us look at what some of the great philosophers have written about the importance of thinking:

"We may divide thinkers into those who think for themselves and those who think through others. The latter are the rule and the former the exception. The first are original thinkers in a double sense, and egotists in the noblest meaning of the word."

—Schopenhauer

"The key to every man is his thought. Sturdy and defiant though he looks he has a helm, which he obeys, which is the idea after which all his facts are classified. He can only be reformed by showing him a new idea which commands his own."

—Emerson

"All truly wise thoughts have been thought already thousands of times; but to make them really ours we must think them over again honestly till they take root in our personal expression."

—Goethe

"All that one is outwardly is but the expression and completion of one's inward—thought. To work effectively one must think clearly. To act nobly one must think nobly."

—Channing

"Great men are they who see that spirituality is stronger than any material force; that thoughts rule the world."

—Emerson

"It is the habitual thought that frames itself into our life. It affects us even more than our intimate social relations do. Our confidential friends have not so much to do in shaping our lives as the thoughts have which we harbor."

—J. W. Teal

Think! Think! Think!

Chapter

17

THE IDEA OF GREATNESS

Too many of us think of great people not as those who serve, but those who succeed in getting others to serve them. They attain positions where they can command others; to exercise power over them, making them obey their will. The exercise of dominion over other people, to most persons, is a great thing. Nothing seems to be sweeter to the selfish soul than this. You will always find every selfish and undeveloped person trying to domineer over others and to exercise control over others. From earliest times, people began to enslave one another. For ages the struggle in war, diplomacy, politics, and government has been aimed at the securing of control over others. Kings and princes have drenched the soil of the earth in blood and tears in the effort to extend their dominions and their power to rule more people.

The struggle of the business world today is the same as that on the battlefields of Europe centuries ago so far as the ruling principle is concerned. It is hard to understand why men like Rockefeller and Carnegie kept seeking more money and made themselves slaves to the business struggle when they already have more than they could possibly use. As one pundit commented, "Suppose a man had fifty thousand pairs of pants, seventy-five thousand vests, one hundred thousand coats, and one hundred and fifty thousand neckties, what would you think of him if he arose in the morning before light and worked until after it was dark every day, rain or shine, in all kinds of weather, merely to get another necktie?"

But there is more to it than just obtaining more possessions. The possession of neckties gives a person no power over others while the possession of dollars does. Rockefeller, Carnegie, and their kind were not after dollars but power. It is the struggle for the high place. It develops able people, cunning people, resourceful people, but not *great* people.

I want you to contrast these two ideas of greatness sharply in your minds. Let me stand before the average American audience and ask the name of the greatest American and the majority will think of Abraham Lincoln. Is this not because in Lincoln above all the other men who have served us in public life we recognize the spirit of service? Not servility, but service. Lincoln was a great man because he knew how to be a great servant. Napoleon, able, cold, selfish, seeking the high places, was a brilliant man. Lincoln was great; Napoleon was not.

The very moment you begin to advance and are recognized as one who is doing things in a great way you will find yourself in danger. The temptation to patronize, advise, or take upon yourself the direction of other people's affairs is sometimes almost irresistible. Avoid, however, the opposite danger of falling into servility, or of completely throwing yourself away in the service of others. To do this has been the ideal of a great many people. Thousands of people have belittled themselves and given up all else to go about doing good – practicing an altruism that is really as morbid and as far from great as the rankest selfishness. The finer instincts which respond to the cry of trouble or distress are not by any means all of you; they are not necessarily the best part of you. There are other things you must do besides helping the unfortunate, although it is true that a large part of the life and activities of every great person must be given to helping other people. As you begin to advance they will come to you. Do not turn them away. But do not make the fatal error of supposing that the life of complete self-abnegation is the way of greatness.

To make another point here, let me refer to the writings of the 18th century Swedish philosopher, Emmanuel Swedenborg. He divided all people into two groups: those who live in pure love, and those who live in what he called the love of ruling for the love of self. Swedenborg saw this selfish love of power as the cause of all sin. It was the only evil desire of the human heart from which all other evil desires sprang. He saw it as the ruling principle in the hells where the spirits of lost people schemed and struggled for dominion over one another, and to enslave one another, just as they had done upon the earth.

Over against this he places pure love. He does not say love of God or love of others, but merely love. Nearly all religionists make more of love and service to God than they do of love and service to humankind. But it is a fact that love of God is not sufficient to save a person from the lust for power. Some of the most ardent lovers of the Deity have been the worst of tyrants. Lovers of God are often tyrants, and lovers of other people are often meddlesome and officious.

Chapter
18

A VIEW OF EVOLUTION

How shall we avoid throwing ourselves into altruistic work if we are surrounded by poverty, ignorance, suffering, and every appearance of misery as very many people are? Those who live where the withered hand of want is thrust upon them from every side appealingly for aid must find it hard to refrain from continuous giving. However, there are social and other irregularities and injustices done to the weak, which fire generous souls with an almost irresistible desire to set things right. We want to start a crusade. We feel that the wrongs will never be righted until we give ourselves wholly to the task. In all this we must fall back upon the point of view. We must remember that this is not a bad world but a good world in the process of becoming.

Beyond all doubt there was a time when there was no life upon this earth. The testimony of geology to the fact that the globe was once a ball of burning gas and molten rock, clothed about with boiling vapors, is indisputable. We do not know how life could have existed under such conditions; that seems impossible. Geology tells us that later on a crust formed, the globe cooled and hardened, the vapors condensed and became mist or fell in rain. The cooled surface crumbled into soil; moisture accumulated; ponds and seas were gathered together, and at last somewhere in the water or on the land appeared something that was alive.

It is reasonable to suppose that this first life was in single-celled organisms, but behind these cells was the insistent urge of Spirit, the Great One Life seeking expression. And soon organisms having too much life to express themselves with one cell had two cells and then many, and still more life was poured into them. Multiple-celled organisms were formed; plants, trees, vertebrates, and mammals, many of them with strange shapes, but all were perfect after their kind as everything is that God makes. No doubt there were crude and almost monstrous forms of both animal and plant life; but everything filled its purpose in its day and it was all very good. Then another day came, the great day of the evolutionary process—the human being, the object aimed at from the beginning, had appeared upon the scene—an ape-like being, little different from the beasts in appearance but infinitely different in the capacity for growth and thought. Art and beauty, architecture and song, poetry and music, all these were unrealized possibilities in the human soul.

From the day the first human appeared God began to put more and more of Himself into each succeeding generation, urging them on to larger achievements and to better conditions, social, governmental, and domestic. Those looking back into ancient history see the awful conditions that existed – barbarities, idolatries, and sufferings. Reading about God in connection with these things, they may be disposed to feel that He was cruel and unjust to humankind. They should pause to think. From the earliest human creatures the race has continued to rise. This could only be accomplished by the successive developments of the various powers and possibilities latent in the human brain. Naturally the cruder and more animal-like parts of humankind came to its full development first. For ages people were brutal; their governments were brutal, their religions were brutal, their domestic institutions were brutal, and what appears to be an immense amount of suffering resulted from this brutality. But God never delighted in suffering, and in every age. He has given us a message, telling us how to avoid it. And all the while the urge

172

of life, insistent, powerful, compelling, made the human race keep moving forward leading to a little less brutality in each age and a little more spirituality in each age.

In every age there have been some individuals who were in advance of the mass and who heard and understood God better than their peers. Upon these the inspiring hand of Spirit was laid and they were compelled to become interpreters. These were the prophets and seers, sometimes the priests and kings, and oftener still they were martyrs driven to the stake, the block, or the cross. It is to these who have heard God, spoken his word, and demonstrated His truth in their lives that all progress is really due.

Again, considering for a moment the presence of what is called evil in the world, we see that that which appears to us to be evil is only undeveloped; and that the undeveloped is perfectly good in its own stage and place. Because all things are necessary to the complete development of human life, all things in human life are the work of God. Even poverty and crime are part of this development. God consciously and voluntarily produced them. They are part of the plan of development that must be played. And when this part has been played, God will sweep them off the stage as He did the strange and poisonous monsters that filled the swamps of the past ages.

In concluding this vision of evolution we might ask why it was all done, what is it for? This question should be easy for the thoughtful mind to answer. God desired to express Himself, to live in form, and not only that, but to live in a form through which He could express Himself on the highest moral and spiritual plane. God wanted to evolve a form in which He could live as a god and manifest Himself as a god. This was the aim of the evolutionary force. The ages of warfare, bloodshed, suffering, injustice, and cruelty were tempered in many ways with love and justice as time advanced. And this was developing the brain of humankind to a point where it should be capable of giving full expression to the love and justice of God. The end is not yet. God aims not at the perfection of a few choice specimens for exhibition, like the large berries at the top of the box, but at the glorification of the race. The time will come when the Kingdom of God shall be established on earth, when there shall be no more crying, no more pain, for the former things are all passed away, and there shall be no night there.

Chapter

19

Serving God

When people start out to make something of themselves and to practice the science of being great, they find themselves necessarily compelled to rearrange many of their relationships. There are friends who perhaps must be alienated; there are relatives who misunderstand and who feel that they are in some way being slighted. The question at the outset is: Is it my duty to make the most of myself regardless of everything else? Or shall I wait until I can do so without any friction or without causing loss to anyone? This is the question of duty to self vs. duty to others.

An immense number of people have a great deal of uncertainty, not to say anxiety, as to what they ought to do for God. The amount of work and service that is done for God by people all over the world through their places of worship and other faith-based organizations is enormous. An immense amount of human energy is expended in what is called serving God. How can we serve God best? Is the conventional idea as to what constitutes service to God all wrong?

The view of evolution that we have taken shows God seeking expression through humankind. Through all the successive ages in which His spirit has urged humans up the height, God has gone on seeking expression. Every generation is more Godlike than the preceding generation. Every generation demands more in the way of fine homes, pleasant surroundings, congenial work, rest, travel, and opportunity for study than the preceding generation.

I have heard some shortsighted economists argue that the working people of today ought surely to be fully contented because their condition is so much better than that of the workers hundreds of years ago who slept in windowless huts on a floor covered with rushes in company with the pigs. If those people had all that they were able to use for the living of all the life they knew how to live, they were perfectly content, and if they lacked what they needed, they were not content. Today's people have comfortable homes and very many things, indeed that were unknown just a short time ago. If they have all that they can use for the living of all the life they can imagine, they will be content. But people are not content. God has lifted the race so far that any person can picture a better and more desirable life than he or she is able to live under existing conditions. As long as this is true, as long as we can think and clearly picture to ourselves a more desirable life, we will be discontented with the life we have to live, and rightly so. That discontent is the Spirit of God urging us on to more desirable conditions.

The only service you can render God is to give expression to what He is trying to give the world, through you. The only service you can render God is to make the very most of yourself in order that God may live in you to the utmost of your possibilities. You may remember the story in the first part of this book about the little girl at the piano, the music in whose soul could not find expression through her untrained hands. This is a good illustration of the way the Spirit of God is over, about, around, and in all of us, seeking to do great things with us, as soon as we will train our hands and feet, our minds, brains, and bodies to do His service.

Your first duty to God, to yourself, and to the world is to make yourself as great a personality, in every way, as you possibly can.

'Do unto others as ye would that they should do unto you' is not too old to use in the New Civilization. Live for all you are worth yourself, but let the others have a chance to live too. This is true success; team work is hard to do perfectly, but if we use our genius, our power, our mastery to help others, and rise in deeper patience and helpfulness to the majesty of our place on the path, then power becomes a wonderful possession, our word never comes back to us void, and we can know that we are the highest expression of our own type of consciousness; that we can command, everything will love to obey, because we are one with all, in truth, in justice, and in power.

In a preceding chapter it was pointed out that it is within the power of all of us to become great just as indicated in the first part of this book, it is within the power of all of us to become rich. But these sweeping generalizations need qualifying. There are people who have such materialistic minds that they are absolutely incapable of comprehending the philosophy set forth in this book. There is a great mass of men and women who have lived and worked until they are practically incapable of thought along these lines; and they cannot receive the message. Something may be done for them by demonstration, that is, by living the life before them. But that is the only way they can be aroused. The world needs demonstration more than it needs teaching. For this mass of people our duty is to become as great in personality as possible in order that they may see and desire to do likewise. It is our duty to make ourselves great for their sakes so that we may help prepare the world that the next generation shall have better conditions for thought.

If you are a person who wishes to make something of yourself and to move out into the world, but are hampered by home ties, having others more or less dependent upon you and whom you fear would suffer if left alone, it is your duty to move out fearlessly, and to make the most of yourself. If there is a loss at home it will be only temporary and apparent, for in a little while, if you follow the leading of Spirit, you will be able to take better care of your dependents than you have ever done before.

Chapter

20

A MENTAL EXERCISE

The purpose of mental exercises must not be misunderstood. There is no virtue in charms or formulated strings of words; there is no short cut to development by repeating prayers or incantations. A mental exercise is an exercise, not in repeating words, but in the thinking of certain thoughts. The phrases that we repeatedly hear become convictions. The thoughts that we repeatedly think become habitual, and make us what we are. The purpose in taking a mental exercise is that you may think certain thoughts repeatedly until you form a habit of thinking them; then they will be your thoughts all the time. Taken in the right way and with an understanding of their purpose, mental exercises are of great value; but taken as most people take them they are worse than useless.

The thoughts embodied in the following exercise are the ones you want to think. You should take the exercise once or twice daily, but you should think the thoughts continuously. That is, do not think them twice a day for a stated time and then forget them until it is time to take the exercise again. The exercise is to impress you with the material for continuous thought.

Take a time when you can have from twenty minutes to half an hour secure from interruption, and proceed first to make yourself physically comfortable Lie at ease in a lounge chair, or on a couch, or in bed; it is best to lie flat on your back. If you have no other time, take the exercise on going to bed at night and before rising in the morning.

First let your attention travel over your body from the crown of your head to the soles of your feet, relaxing every muscle as you go. Relax completely. And next, get physical and other ills off your mind. Let the attention pass down the spinal cord and out over the nerves to the extremities, and as you do so think: "My nerves are in perfect order all over my body. They obey my will, and I have great nerve force."

Next, bring your attention to the lungs and think: "I am breathing deeply and quietly, and the air goes into every cell of my lungs, which are in perfect condition. My blood is purified and made clean."

Next, to the heart: "My heart is beating strongly and steadily, and my circulation is perfect, even to the extremities."

Next, to the digestive system: "My stomach and bowels perform their work perfectly. My food is digested and assimilated and my body rebuilt and nourished. My liver, kidneys, and bladder each perform their several functions without pain or strain; I am perfectly well. My body is resting, my mind is quiet, and my soul is at peace."

"I have no anxiety about financial or other matters. God, who is within me, is also in all things I want, impelling them toward me; all that I want is already given to me. I have no anxiety about my health, for I am perfectly well. I have no worry or fear whatever.

"I rise above all temptation to moral evil. I cast out all greed, selfishness, and narrow personal ambition; I do not hold envy, malice, or enmity toward any living soul. I will follow no course of action that is not in accord with my highest ideals. I am right and I will do right."

VIEWPOINT

"All is right with the world. It is perfect and advancing to completion. I will contemplate the facts of social, political, and industrial life only from this high viewpoint. Behold, it is all very good. I will see all human beings, my acquaintances, friends, neighbors, and the members of my own household in the same way. They are good. Nothing is wrong with the universe; nothing can be wrong but my own personal attitude, and henceforth I keep that right. My whole trust is in God."

CONSECRATION

"I will obey my soul and be true to that within me that is highest. I search within for the pure idea of right in all things, and when I find it, I will express it in my outward life. I will abandon everything I have outgrown for the best I can think. I will have the highest thoughts concerning all my relationships, and my manner and action shall express these thoughts. I surrender my body to be ruled by my mind; I yield my mind to the dominion of my soul, and I give my soul to the guidance of God."

IDENTIFICATION

"There is but one substance and source, and of that I am made and with it I am one. It is God. I proceeded forth and came from it. God and I are one, and God is greater than I, and I do His will. I surrender myself to conscious unity with Pure Spirit; there is but one and that one is everywhere. I am one with the Eternal Consciousness."

IDEALIZATION

Form a mental picture of yourself as you want to be, and at the greatest height your imagination can picture. Dwell upon this for some little time, holding the thought: "This is what I really am; it is a picture of my own soul. I am this now in soul, and I am becoming this in outward manifestation."

REALIZATION

"I appropriate to myself the power to become what I want to be, and to do what I want to do. I exercise creative energy; all the power there is is mine. I will arise and go forth with power and perfect confidence; I will do mighty works in the strength of the Lord, my God. I will trust and not fear, for God is with me."

Chapter
21

A Summary of The Science of Being Great

All human beings are made of the one intelligent substance, and therefore all contain the same essential powers and possibilities. Greatness is equally inherent in all, and may be manifested by all. Every person may become great. Every constituent of God is a constituent of humankind.

We may overcome both heredity and circumstances by exercising the inherent creative power of the soul. If we are to become great, the soul must act, and must rule the mind and the body. Our knowledge is limited, and we fall into error through ignorance; to avoid this we must connect our soul with Universal Spirit.

Universal Spirit is the intelligent substance from which all things come. It is in and through all things. All things are known to this universal mind, and we can so unite ourselves with it as to enter into all knowledge.

To do this we must cast out of ourselves everything, which separates us from God. We must will to live the divine life, and we must rise above all moral temptations. We must forsake every course of action that is not in accord with our highest ideals.

We must reach the right viewpoint, recognizing that God is all, in all, and that there is nothing wrong. We must see that nature, society, government, and industry are perfect in their present stage, and advancing toward completion—that all men and women everywhere are good and perfect. We must know that all is right with the world, and unite with God for the completion of the perfect work. It is only as we see God as the Great Advancing Presence in all, and good in all, that we can rise to real greatness.

We must consecrate ourselves to the service of the highest that is within ourselves, obeying the voice of the soul. There is an Inner Light in each of us, which continuously impels us toward the highest, and we must be guided by this light if we would become great.

We must recognize the fact that we are one with God, and consciously affirm this unity for ourselves and for all others. We must know the Eternal One to be a god among gods, and act accordingly. We must have absolute faith in our own perceptions of truth, and begin at home to act upon these perceptions. As we see the true and right course in small things, we must take that course. We must cease to act unthinkingly, and begin to think; and we must be sincere in our thoughts.

We must form a mental conception of ourselves at the highest, and hold this conception until it is our habitual thought-form of ourselves. This thought-form must be kept continuously in view. We must outwardly realize and express that thought-form in our actions. We must do everything that we do in a great way. In dealing with family, neighbors, acquaintances, and friends, we must make every act an expression of our ideal.

Once we have reached the right viewpoint, make full consecration, and fully idealize ourselves as great, and make every act, however trivial, an expression of the ideal, we have already attained greatness.

Everything we do will be done in a great way. We will make ourselves known, and will be recognized as a personality of power. We will receive knowledge by inspiration, and will know all that we need to know. We will receive all the material wealth we form in our thoughts, and will not lack for any good thing. We will be given ability to deal with any combination of circumstances that may arise, and our growth and progress will be continuous and rapid. Great works will seek us out, and all will delight to do us honor.